WEALTH AND POWER IN AMERICA
An Analysis of Social Class and Income Distribution

Wealth and Power in America

An Analysis of Social Class and Income Distribution

GABRIEL KOLKO

FREDERICK A. PRAEGER, *Publisher*

New York

BOOKS THAT MATTER

Published in the United States of America in 1962 by
Frederick A. Praeger, Inc., Publisher
64 University Place, New York 3, N.Y.

Printed in the United States of America

To

Joyce

Preface

When a choice must be made between unproved impressions and objective statistics, even a confirmed scoffer will grant that there is no real contest. Yet in the study of the distribution of wealth in the United States—a field in which statistics are abundant—the only large-scale generalizations have been made by people who have no expert knowledge of the subject. Instead, these generalizations have come from the advocates of the income-redistribution thesis, who in nearly every case have based their doctrines—and dominant social theories of our time—on very casual and secondary information.

It is my contention that their theories, which herald a redistribution of wealth and the decline of poverty, have no justification in fact. In my critical evaluation, the American economy has largely failed to attain those equalitarian economic goals that have been a part of our democratic heritage since Jefferson and Jackson.

More than enough is known of the distribution of wealth and of the nature and extent of poverty to examine these topics in a factual, analytical manner. Such an enterprise is long overdue.

Although the data used in this study have been almost wholly unavailable to the general public, they have been readily accessible to social scientists. Since the latter, however, have not exploited them, their use here will be largely new. The analyses I have made depend on a synthesis of the technical work of many scholars in addition to my own research. I have endeavored to present all data in the simplest, most informative and significant manner possible. I have tried to avoid the obscurity that is often mistaken for scholarly profundity. However, depth and seriousness have not been sacrificed for the superficial or the unproved. Any serious and, at points, patient layman should fully understand this book.

Anyone seeking to discover in existing studies the nature of income and wealth distribution in the United States is forced to wade through countless monographs whose only common ground is a concern for methodological technicalities and limitations. This concern, despite the justification for a good part of it, has deadened the study of income distribution to the point that, as one economist has confessed, its major preoccupation is "torturing statistics." There do exist, however, some problems purely methodological in nature, and when they could not be avoided, they have been dealt with here in as nontechnical a manner as possible.

The major problem in the study of the distribution of wealth, however, has not been a technical one. There have been, after all, scores of scholarly tomes, and these have settled most of the outstanding technical problems. Instead, the chief stumbling block has been a paralysis, a reluctance to enter into dispute. "Perhaps in higher degree than in other areas of research," observed Dorothy S. Brady, an income-distribution expert, "the temptation to avoid controversy and to leave firmly entrenched concepts alone has had a stultifying effect. . . . The government worker is not alone in hesitating to make a decision that may bring down the wrath of a powerful group upon his agency." Clearly it is time for an end to such an attitude.

I am in debt to Mulford Q. Sibley for his encouragement and critical insights and to Norman Thomas for valuable questions that prodded me into investigating relevant new areas. Norman Birnbaum and Seymour Melman gave invaluable aid, for which I am most grateful. I, of course, assume all responsibility for statements of opinion or fact. To my wife, Joyce Kolko, I owe a debt that mere words cannot express. This book is in every sense a joint enterprise, and the first in a series of critical studies on which we are presently engaged.

GABRIEL KOLKO

CONTENTS

WEALTH AND POWER IN AMERICA

Introduction

Most recent studies of American society assume that since the end of the Great Depression, in 1939, the nation's wealth has been redistributed and prosperity has been extended to the vast majority of the population. The authors of these works—popular and academic alike—are virtually unanimous in their conviction that our society has attained a substantial measure of social and economic democracy. They hail our economy for its triumphs in eliminating poverty and in creating the life of abundance for the many, not the few.

This assumption of economic equality has become the foundation of broad new theories in the social sciences, the common impression of millions of intelligent laymen—and even the basis of specific political and social policies on taxes, aid to the elderly, poverty, and other areas of economic significance.

But this assumption is nonetheless fallacious, for despite the obvious increase in prosperity since the abysmal years of the Great Depression, the basic distribution of income and wealth in the United States is essentially the same now as it was in 1939, or even 1910. Most low-income groups live substantially better today, but even though their real wages have mounted, their percentage of the national income has not changed.

Furthermore, the economic gains made by the low-income groups have been greatly exaggerated by social commentators. They have, in fact, been guilty of coloring their discussions of American society since 1939 with unwarranted optimism and complacency. At the same time, they have ignored or overlooked the many chronic economic problems—including periodic unemployment, depressed areas, and low-wage industries—that have persisted into the postwar years and continue to threaten the poorly paid. Also, these authorities have failed to recognize the serious economic consequences of numerous social and occupational trends that have been developing over the past two decades. Already, these mounting forces are partly nullifying wage rises, Social Security benefits, and the like. Among these economically significant patterns are the increase in nonunionized white-collar occupations, whose low wage scales are not keeping up with inflation; the rapid enlargement of the old-age population, a traditionally low-income group; and the sharp rise divorce and separation has caused in the number of households headed by women, another traditionally low-income group.

The impact of these new and old causes of poverty can be measured statistically: well over one-third of the nation's households subsist on incomes too meager to provide minimum standards of health and decency. Such conditions exist not only in poor states like Mississippi and West Virginia, but also in New York, one of the states with the greatest wealth per capita. It follows inevitably that because of the disproportionately small share of the national income received by the low-income population, this group consumes a disproportionately small share of all forms of goods, including housing, education, and medical care.

And yet, in the midst of this somber economic reality, a myth has sprung up about across-the-board prosperity in America. "The democratization of our economic system" is hailed by Frederick Lewis Allen in *The Big Change* (1952).[1] The "proof" of this so-called democratization is the widespread—and scientifically unsound—claim that, as economist Joseph Spengler puts it, "available statistical data indicate that over-all income inequality in the United States has been diminishing since the late 1920's."[2] The next logical assertion arising from this myth is that the assumed equalization of income has brought about greater equality in consumption and in possession of the symbols of economic status. David Riesman traces this transition in *The Lonely Crowd* (1953), theorizing that an "abundance psychology" evolves from a "scarcity psychology" as "the distributive machinery of society improves in terms of both income distribution and goods distribution."[3] He projects the lessening inequalities in consumption and status resulting from income differentials and foresees the eventual disappearance of social classes founded on these inequalities.

The fabricators of this myth of America as a mass, nearly classless society in the consumption of goods have, as we have seen above, based their notions on the erroneous belief that major changes have been effected in the American economy. They have not suggested that a society could radically transform its class and status system without altering its economic foundations.

To the extent that these observers have considered the economic basis of "the big change," they have relied on the impressive statistical work of Simon Kuznets, in *Shares of Upper Income Groups in Income and Savings,* published in 1953 by the National Bureau of Economic Research. This book concerns only the wealthiest 5 per cent of the population and its share of the nation's income, but it has provided the foundation for sweeping theories concerning American society as a whole. Clearly, a study that ignores the economic lives of the remaining 95 per cent of the population is far too limited.

We shall consider in the following pages to what degree America is, as John Kenneth Galbraith asserts, an "affluent society." And we shall evaluate the belief, expressed by David Lilienthal in *Big Business: A New Era* (1953), that "today one finds the physical benefits of our society distributed widely, to almost everyone, with scant regard to status, class or origin of the individual."[4] We shall do so by examining factual data regarding the extent and causes of poverty and low incomes. This study will also enable us to predict whether poverty will rise or decline in the near future and whether a high level of consumption and prosperity is possible for all classes even within the economy's framework of unequal incomes.

We shall also scrutinize the conclusion of economic historian Shepard B. Clough, in *The American Way* (1953), that the "progress which has been made in the last twenty years toward a more equitable sharing in the benefits of economic growth shows what is possible under the capitalist system."[5] Surprisingly, there has been almost no previous attempt to test whether, in fact, any redistribution of income and wealth has taken place.

In our statistical examination of all these issues, we shall do more than assess the dominant social theory of our time. We shall also discover the outlines of the actual American class structure that emerges from the inequalities of income, wealth, and economic power. The dimensions of class obviously include more than economics—there are also cultural, racial, and other factors—but economics is probably the most pervasive and important. A family's existence is quite predictably circumscribed by its economic boundaries; non-economic factors can create diversity only with those limits. However, the prolific research devoted to the lesser distinctions has overshadowed the more significant—and almost totally ignored—economic basis of class, a distortion I shall endeavor to correct.

Thomas Jefferson feared and distrusted "an aristocracy of wealth [as] of more harm and danger than benefit to society." Traditionally, it has been recognized that the danger of excessive concentration of wealth arises from the economic power it brings. This has an enormous potential; it can be used to influence the mass media, to affect the political order, to stimulate economic cycles—to name just a few of its consequences. Although the equalitarian goal has never been challenged as an American ideal, the economic revolution that followed the Civil War brought the economy largely under the control of a small number of individuals who acquired vast fortunes and economic power. Sharing Jefferson's fear and accepting his goal, advocates of the income-redistribution theory rejoice that the post-Civil War inequities have been righted. But it is highly questionable whether the economic power arising from the possession or control of savings, economic assets, and income, and a voice in corporate policy has become more diffused since the early days of the New Deal. Now, when political democracy is challenged by a totalitarian way of life that also holds out the promise of economic equality, it is of crucial importance for us to evaluate the structure of the American economy and decide whether it has, in fact, achieved the equalitarian goal set forth by Jefferson.

1

Trends in the Distribution of Income

The social scientist inquiring into the distribution of income in America finds his task of obtaining accurate information complicated in two significant ways by the expansion of the Federal tax system over the past two decades. Since he is seeking the same information as the tax collector, he is confronted with essentially the same barriers of deception and silence in approaching an important segment of the population, including a good number of the very wealthy. Also, he must devise ways of measuring the ingenious forms of income created by the wealthy in their efforts to minimize their taxes. Thus, he must evaluate expense-account allowances, corporate profits not paid out to stockholders, and personal earnings to be paid at a deferred date, as well as various forms of interest, dividend, and other income not appearing in existing data. In the lower-income brackets, a form of income he must take into account is home-grown food.

If, then, the social scientist is resourceful and tenacious in his research and avoids confusing illusion with reality, he will finally have revealed the unvarnished, if complicated, reality of the present-day distribution of income in the United States.

In studying the major trends in the distribution of income,

we shall consider the nation's population as an aggregate of families and unattached individuals ranked according to the size of their annual income. We shall then divide them, from top to bottom, into ten groups, each containing the same number of families and unattached individuals. These will be referred to as income-tenths.

Since much of the recent research on income distribution has been done in terms of income-fifths, my departure from this approach may demand some justification. I have two major objections to discussing income distribution by fifths of the population: First, such statistics extend back only as far as 1935–36. Second, these larger units obscure important patterns of income distribution that appear only when the population is further divided into tenths.

The conventional way of discussing income distribution is to take the whole range of personal incomes, break it down into consecutive income brackets, and then determine the percentage of families and unrelated individuals that belongs in each division. This approach was used, for instance, by a *New York Times* financial writer when he explained that "where three out of four families had incomes of less than $2,000 a year in 1939, only one out of three fell into that class ten years later."[1] As in this case, studies of income distribution based on income-size frequently ignore the role of inflation in raising dollar incomes and producing an upward shift in the distribution—those near the top of one income class are pushed into the lower levels of the next-highest class. These inflation-caused ascents in income-size distributions are absolutely unrelated to any increases in the real income—the purchasing power—of the population. For example, a family of four earning $3,000 in 1946 and earning $4,445 in 1958 had merely maintained the identical real income. From 1947 through 1958, the average American family income increased 50 per cent in dollars, but the size of this jump shrinks if one knows that 32 of these percentage points are merely the result of inflation; only 18 of the percentage points indicate greater purchasing power.[2] However, when income-size distribution figures are corrected to eliminate the inflationary content, they are well suited for the study of changes in real income. More important, from our point of view, the changes in income-size distribution generally tell us little about the proportionate distribution of income among the population. A rise in the real income of a group does not itself indicate an increase in its percentage of the national income. In fact, an income group can enjoy a boost in real wages while simultaneously suffering a loss in its percentage of the country's income. A failure to distinguish between these two separate concepts is the basic flaw in the theory that the rising standard of living of the past few decades has been accompanied by a trend toward equalization in the percentage of the country's income earned by each tenth or fifth of the population. This failure to distinguish is illustrated in a statement by economist Henry C. Wallich of Yale University that recent changes in the income distribution "reflect both a great improvement in the over-all standard of living and also a cutting of the economic pie into servings of more nearly equal size."[3] Such a merging of two distinct issues only obscures the nature of the changes that have occurred since 1933.

A COMPARISON OF METHODS

The abundance of data on income distribution collected by different methods over the past several decades makes a comparison of their value essential. Their only common characteristic is their failure, because of understatement and nonreporting by taxpayers or interviewees, to calculate the distribution of the entire national personal money income. Studies show that the Survey Research Center data (prepared

until 1959 for the Federal Reserve Board) accounted for
anywhere from 77 to 95 per cent of the total, the U.S. Bureau
of the Census has accounted for 74 to 81 per cent, and individual income-tax returns have accounted for 86 to 91 per
cent.[4]

Census calculations of income-size distributions attempt to
cover all money income except capital gains, and exclude
nonmoney income-in-kind, such as home-produced food and
fuel, the rental value of owner-occupied homes, wages in the
form of food and services, free bank services, and certain
nondeclared interest. The Office of Business Economics of
the Department of Commerce, in its studies of income distribution by size and by income-fifths, includes all money
income and many forms of income-in-kind, but it excludes
undistributed profits, most expense-account allowances, and
many forms of unreported income. The Survey Research
Center data on income distribution by size and income-tenths
covers money income only.

These agencies also differ in their definition of family units
or households. The Survey Research Center uses a "spending
unit," consisting of all related persons living in the same
dwelling who pool their incomes. Husband, wife, and children under eighteen years living at home are always in the
same unit. Other relatives in the household are separate units
if they earn more than $15 a week and do not pool their
incomes. Persons living in institutions, military reservations,
hotels, or large rooming houses are excluded. The National
Industrial Conference Board "recipient unit" includes all
related persons who live in the same dwelling. It ignores
second breadwinners, but since before 1941 their earnings
were very low, this would not seriously affect the basic pattern of income distribution.[5] The Census uses the "family,"
defined as two or more related individuals living together,
irrespective of how they treat their income, and "unrelated
individuals," defined as persons who do not live with their

family, but who may live with other "unrelated individuals." Only persons living in institutions or military reservations are excluded. The Office of Business Economics "consumer unit" is used to indicate either the family or unrelated individuals as defined by the Census, and also excludes only persons living in institutions or military reservations.[6] All these methodological variations, however, are a relatively minor consideration. A much more important problem is the failure of individuals to report their total income. These omissions are so substantial that their inclusion in existing statistics would necessitate a thorough reappraisal of all previous conclusions on income distribution.

The Survey Research Center figures for income distribution by tenths, compiled from 1941 through 1959, are more reliable than either Census or Federal income-tax data, because they are obtained directly from the heads of households, who disclose information more freely in an anonymous situation to a nongovernmental agency than they do to the Federal bureaus. Consequently, the Survey figures usually account for a relatively high percentage of the national money income.[7] Prior to 1941, the best material on income distribution by tenths was compiled by the National Industrial Conference Board. Like the Survey, it excludes income-in-kind, but this, again, can be adjusted.

THE UNCHANGING PATTERN OF INEQUALITY

A radically unequal distribution of income has been characteristic of the American social structure since at least 1910, and despite minor year-to-year fluctuations in the shares of the income-tenths, no significant trend toward income equality has appeared. This, in brief, is the deduction that can be made from a study of Table I, on page 14.

Throughout the 1950's, the income of the top tenth was larger than the total for the bottom five income-tenths—

TABLE I

PERCENTAGE OF NATIONAL PERSONAL INCOME, BEFORE TAXES,
RECEIVED BY EACH INCOME-TENTH*

	Highest Tenth	2nd	3rd	4th	5th	6th	7th	8th	9th	Lowest Tenth
1910	33.9	12.3	10.2	8.8	8.0	7.0	6.0	5.5	4.9	3.4
1918	34.5	12.9	9.6	8.7	7.7	7.2	6.9	5.7	4.4	2.4
1921	38.2	12.8	10.5	8.9	7.4	6.5	5.9	4.6	3.2	2.0
1929	39.0	12.3	9.8	9.0	7.9	6.5	5.5	4.6	3.6	1.8
1934	33.6	13.1	11.0	9.4	8.2	7.3	6.2	5.3	3.8	2.1
1937	34.4	14.1	11.7	10.1	8.5	7.2	6.0	4.4	2.6	1.0
1941	34.0	16.0	12.0	10.0	9.0	7.0	5.0	4.0	2.0	1.0
1945	29.0	16.0	13.0	11.0	9.0	7.0	6.0	5.0	3.0	1.0
1946	32.0	15.0	12.0	10.0	9.0	7.0	6.0	5.0	3.0	1.0
1947	33.5	14.8	11.7	9.9	8.5	7.1	5.8	4.4	3.1	1.2
1948	30.9	14.7	11.9	10.1	8.8	7.5	6.3	5.0	3.3	1.4
1949	29.8	15.5	12.5	10.6	9.1	7.7	6.2	4.7	3.1	0.8
1950	28.7	15.4	12.7	10.8	9.3	7.8	6.3	4.9	3.2	0.9
1951	30.9	15.0	12.3	10.6	8.9	7.6	6.3	4.7	2.9	0.8
1952	29.5	15.3	12.4	10.6	9.1	7.7	6.4	4.9	3.1	1.0
1953	31.4	14.8	11.9	10.3	8.9	7.6	6.2	4.7	3.0	1.2
1954	29.3	15.3	12.4	10.7	9.1	7.7	6.4	4.8	3.1	1.2
1955	29.7	15.7	12.7	10.8	9.1	7.7	6.1	4.5	2.7	1.0
1956	30.6	15.3	12.3	10.5	9.0	7.6	6.1	4.5	2.8	1.3
1957	29.4	15.5	12.7	10.8	9.2	7.7	6.1	4.5	2.9	1.3
1958	27.1	16.3	13.2	11.0	9.4	7.8	6.2	4.6	3.1	1.3
1959	28.9	15.8	12.7	10.7	9.2	7.8	6.3	4.6	2.9	1.1

* In terms of "recipients" for 1910–37 and "spending units" for 1941–59.

Source: Data for 1910–37 are from National Industrial Conference Board, *Studies in Enterprise and Social Progress* (New York: National Industrial Conference Board, 1939), p. 125. Data for 1941–59 were calculated by the Survey Research Center. Figures for 1941–46 are available in rounded form only. Previously unpublished data for 1947–58 are reproduced by permission of the Board of Governors of the Federal Reserve System, and data for 1959 by permission of the Survey Research Center.

about the same relationship as existed in 1910 and 1918. The income share of the richest tenth has dropped only slightly, if at all, since 1910. The average percentage of the national personal income before taxes, received by this group was about one-eighth less in 1950–59 than in 1910–41, omitting the exceptional years 1921 and 1929. This loss, however, disappears when the 1950–59 figures are corrected to allow for their exclusion of all forms of income-in-kind and the very substantial understatement of income by the wealthy, both of which are consequences of the post-1941 expansion in income taxation.

While the income share of the richest tenth has remained large and virtually constant over the past half century, the two lowest income-tenths have experienced a sharp decline. In 1910, the combined income shares of the two poorest income-tenths were about one-quarter that of the richest tenth; by 1959, their share had dropped to one-seventh. During this same period, the percentage of the next-lowest tenth also decreased, while the fourth and fifth from the lowest tenths (the sixth- and seventh-ranking) neither gained nor lost ground appreciably. Together these five groups, which constitute the poorer half of the U.S. population, received 27 per cent of the national personal income in 1910, but only 23 per cent in 1959. Thus, for the only segments of the population in which a gain could indicate progress toward economic democracy, there has been no increase in the percentage share of the national income.

The only significant rises in income distribution have occurred in the second- and third-richest income-tenths. Their combined shares increased more than one-quarter from 1910 to 1959, and by the end of that period their combined income share was almost equal to that of the richest tenth. It should be noted, however, that their gain was made almost entirely during the Depression years of the 1930's. Further, this group is largely made up of persons in occupations such as professionals, small businessmen, top clerical workers, and lesser managers, with rising salary or wage incomes and low unemployment, and by no means was in urgent need of a greater share of the national income.

Many recent explanations of rising real and dollar incomes

in the lower-income groups since 1939 or 1941, which have been utilized to prove the occurrence of a radical and purportedly permanent income redistribution, ignore the fact that these increases reflect increased employment, not an alteration in the basic distribution structure.

Prior to World War II, it was commonly assumed that the different phases of the business cycle affected the distribution of income—that relative income inequality rose when unemployment rose. However, the relationship between employment trends and income is more important in the study of real income and dollar earnings than in the study of income distribution. During an upward trend in unemployment, the *dollar earnings* of the lowest-income classes decline much more rapidly than those of the other groups, and during an upswing in employment, both the dollar earnings and real income of the lowest-income classes rise much more rapidly than those of the higher-income groups. During full employment, the rate at which the dollar income of the poorer classes increases generally keeps pace with the rate of rise for the highest classes (although occasionally falling slightly behind—as from 1948 to the early 1950's).[8]

However, even the pre-1941 data show that once common generalizations on the correlation between employment trends and income distribution did not always hold true. The income share of the highest tenth increased sharply in 1929, during a period of only moderately high employment. More important, even in the period of comparative full employment since 1941, the income shares of the poorer half of the nation have either declined or remained stable.

EXPENSE ACCOUNTS—INCOME-IN-KIND FOR
CORPORATE EXECUTIVES

Material on money income must be supplemented by data on distribution of income-in-kind among income classes to arrive at more nearly accurate figures for total income and income inequality.

Extensive data show that in 1941 the total dollar value of income-in-kind for urban families was relatively insignificant, ranging from $155 for families earning less than $500, to $457 for those earning more than $10,000. For farm families, income-in-kind ranged in value from $417 for those earning less than $500, to $719 for those earning more than $3,000. Each tenth of farm consumer-units received roughly the same value in home-produced food, but the richest third received about one-half the rental value in housing.[9] Thus, except for those with extremely small earnings, income-in-kind was only a minor factor in farm incomes in 1941.

In the ensuing twenty years, the value of home-grown food has been declining consistently for the farmer, from about one-fifth of his cash income in 1941, to about one-tenth in the early postwar period. The farmer purchased 28 per cent of his total food consumption in 1923; he purchased 60 per cent in 1955. The farm population has declined radically since World War II, and its share of the national disposable income since 1945 dropped by more than half, to 3.7 per cent in 1956; and in 1957 farm food- and fuel-in-kind was equal to only 0.5 per cent of the national personal income. Clearly, the role of farm income-in-kind in the national income distribution is now of no great importance.[10]

Among urban consumers in the lowest tenths, income-in-kind has been mainly relief goods, and these have become inconsequential with the advent of full—if sporadically so—employment.

Meanwhile, as income-in-kind declined in value for farm and low-income families, it gained new prominence in the highest income-tenth, and especially the top 5 per cent of the spending units. Here it takes the form of the expense account and other executive benefits. A by-product of the steeper Federal personal and corporate tax rates instituted in 1941, the expense account is now an acknowledged form of executive remuneration. In 1959, a Harvard Business School study revealed that two-thirds of corporate executives regarded their expense accounts as tax-free compensation. Legally, a corporation can deduct as expenses only bills incurred in the "ordinary and necessary" course of business, but the fact that a corporation in the top tax bracket is only 48 cents out of pocket for every dollar it deducts from its Federal tax bill has led to some broad interpretations of business costs. Especially at the extremes, in closely owned or very widely diffused corporations, extravagant use has been made of income-in-kind for management. The *Wall Street Journal* frequently mentions such items as $300-a-day hotel suites, $10,000-to-$25,000 parties, executive penthouses with marble walls and gold faucets. According to one *Wall Street Journal* report: "Hidden hunting lodges are one of the 'fringe benefits' awaiting officials who succeed in working their way up to the executive suite of a good many U.S. corporations. Other impressive prizes: sharing use of yachts, private planes and railroad cars, jaunts to exotic watering places and spectacular soirées—all paid for by the corporation. . . . Companies maintaining private retreats, planes and other facilities for fun or luxurious traveling generally report they are necessary to the conduct of their business. . . . This is the prime reason for some companies maintaining such facilities, though perhaps not for others. Even in the former case, executives generally manage to get considerable enjoyment from their firms' luxury properties. . . . In this way, a good many executives whose fortune-building efforts are impaired by today's high taxes still are enjoying the frills enjoyed by the Mellons, Morgans and Baruchs."[11]

Company-provided luxuries are obvious indicators of a man's position in the hierarchy. For the top corporate elite, they generally include a company car, a gas credit card, vacations, excellent medical care, country-club memberships, dining and entertainment, and the cash difference between expense allowances and actual expenditures. Lesser corporate personnel receive lesser benefits, according to their rank.

In 1954, 37 per cent of the Cadillacs registered in Manhattan and 20 per cent of those registered in Philadelphia were in the names of businesses. Some 80 per cent of the check totals of the most expensive restaurants and 30 to 40 per cent of Broadway theater tickets are covered by expense accounts. Most of the items charged to Diners' Club, American Express, and other luxury credit-card clubs by members, who numbered well over a million in 1958, are paid for by businesses.[12]

One-half of the executives in small companies and one-third of those in large companies are reimbursed for their expenses in social clubs and organizations. More than one-half of the executives in small firms and more than one-quarter of those in large companies are provided with private automobiles. One-fifth of the large corporations have their own country clubs and resorts for their executives.

Gifts received by executives—particularly those influential in purchasing—from personnel in other corporations are another type of income-in-kind. For Christmas, 1959, such giving accounted for $300 million—all tax deductible as business expenses.

Since nearly two-fifths of the top executives do not have to account to anyone for their expenses, and more than three-fifths are given no yardsticks to limit themselves, it is possible for executives to treat themselves to unusual indulgences, and from time to time some of these are revealed to the public—often in the form of advice on expense-account opportunities as suggested in the pages of business publications. One corporation president spent $17,000 of company funds on an African safari; another charged to business expenses $65,000 in jewelry, $22,000 in liquor, $35,000 in night-club tabs, $25,000 in gifts, and $16,000 in boat outlays.

In scope and value, the income-in-kind of the rich presents a sharp contrast to the surplus flour, corn meal, rice, and butter provided as relief goods to the poor.[13]

An unofficial Treasury Department estimate in August, 1957, placed the annual total for corporate expense-account outlays at more than $5 billion, and possibly as high as $10 billion.[14] Certainly a portion of this total was in reality income-in-kind received by members of the top income-tenth. If only one-third of this amount is considered income-in-kind for the top tenth, it would add at least 1 percentage point to this group's share of the national income in 1956.

Although existing statistics do not allow us to calculate precisely the percentage of total expense-account outlays that represent personal income-in-kind, they are sufficient to indicate that income-in-kind was an item of major consequence to the share of the top income-tenth, especially to the style of living enjoyed by many of the richest members of the economic elite.

EVASIONS AND ERRORS: $30 BILLION-PLUS

The existing data on income distribution fail to account for a significant proportion of money income because of underreporting on tax returns and nonreporting to interviewers. Since automatic payroll deductions withhold the amount of money due for Federal income taxes, persons wholly dependent on wages or salary for their incomes—and this includes the vast majority of urban low- and middle-income earners—have little reason to underreport their incomes to data collectors. Whatever payroll earnings are underreported or nonreported are probably to be found in very small companies where executives or owners are in a position to alter their required earnings statements.

However, professionals, businessmen, and others receiving cash payments for their services are in an especially advantageous position to underreport their income on tax returns. Roughly one-half of unreported entrepreneurial income represented farm income, the better part of which probably went to low-income earners.[15] The unreported half going to businessmen and professionals probably went to those already earning enough to underreport their incomes without arousing the suspicion of tax auditors. The result is ultimately indicative of an understatement of income by the upper tenths in tax and other statistics.

Refusal to report income data to interviewers also leads to an understating of income by the highest groups. Nonreporting is almost exclusively confined to the upper brackets. A 1941 Bureau of Labor Statistics study found that "the nonreporting rate tended to be higher in blocks with higher rent levels and with larger proportions of families at upper-income levels, ranging from about 1 per cent at the under $1,000 level to 35 per cent at the $10,000 and over level."[16]

Nondeclaration of income to avoid taxes is illegal, but it is so widespread that no study of income distribution can ignore it. Between 1950 and 1953, the number of Federal income-tax returns reporting high incomes *declined,* a fact that the National Bureau of Economic Research, in view of "the almost certain increase in upper bracket salaries," found "puzzling" and meriting "close investigation."[17]

In 1957, only 91 per cent of the national personal money income was reported on individual income-tax returns, somewhat more than the 86 per cent for 1944–46. The missing sum for 1957—$27.7 billion—comprised 3 per cent ($7.1 billion) of wages and salaries paid, 14 per cent ($1.6 billion) of distributed dividends, 58 per cent ($5.5 billion) of interest, and 27 per cent ($10.8 billion) of entrepreneurial income— the income of nonsalaried professionals, unincorporated businesses, and farmers.[18] About the same amount of personal income is unreported in Census and Survey Research Center data. Obviously, the omission of income of this magnitude—

especially if a large segment of it belongs in any single income-tenth—could produce a crucial distortion in the resulting income-distribution figures.

In 1952, spending units earning more than $10,000 owned more than 80 per cent of the publicly held stock. So it is highly probable that spending units in the top tenth—in that year, those earning more than $7,090—received most of the unreported dividend income.[19] The Bureau of Internal Revenue's sample audit of 1948 tax returns showed that those reporting $25,000-plus in income accounted for 7.2 per cent of all returns with dividend errors and 38.4 per cent of the dollar value of all errors, and that those reporting $7,000-plus in income accounted for 40.7 per cent of all returns with dividend errors and 73.6 per cent of the dollar value of all errors.[20] Most interest-bearing savings, bonds, notes, etc., are owned by the top income-tenth, and thus a large segment of undeclared income in this category must be allocated to the economic elite. The 1948 tax audit found 52.6 per cent of the dollar value of interest errors in the returns for the $7,000-plus bracket, the top income-tenth.[21]

A good part of the existing income-distribution statistics fails to account for income earned in the corporate sector of the economy and—quite legally—not distributed to the owners of stock because of their desire to avoid high tax rates. But any nondistribution of corporate profits directly affects the income of the top income-tenth—especially of that small group within it that, as I will later show in detail, owns the vast bulk of stock. The relative importance of dividends grows with income, and above the $100,000 level, dividends are substantially larger than salary or wages. Since tax avoidance has become a primary concern of the highest income classes, especially since 1941, corporations increasingly retain dividends instead of distributing them. As Harvard economist William Crum has put it, "A group of wealthy directors owning stock in a closely held corporation may vote to retain earnings not so much because of the needs of the business as on account of the large surtaxes for which they would be personally liable were these earnings disbursed."[22] In 1923–29, corporations withheld 27 per cent of their net profits; in 1946–59 the figure was 51 per cent.[23] Had 1946–59 corporate profits been distributed at the 1923–29 rate, an average of $4.7 billion more in dividends would have been paid out annually to individuals, nearly all of them in the top income-tenth.

In this way, the economic elite can spread their dividend incomes evenly during fluctuations in the business cycle. Or they can increase the market value of their stock; then, if they sell it in the future, they will pay taxes on their profits at the much lower capital-gains rate. Corporations themselves have furthered this policy of personal tax avoidance since 1941 by sharply increased understatement and nonreporting of profits, accomplished by such devices as charging capital expenditures to current income. Thus the corporations represent vast income reserves for the economic elite.[24]

If 1950 corporate profits had been distributed at the 1923–29 rate, the top income-tenth would have received 32 per cent rather than 29 per cent of the personal income. For 1952, they would have received 30 per cent rather than 29 per cent. In any postwar year, profits undistributed after allowing for a reasonable rate of corporate savings and self-financing would have added 1 to 4 percentage points to the share of the richest tenth. The value of corporate expense-account income-in-kind would have added at least 1 percentage point. Undeclared income, very conservatively assigning only one-third to one-half of it to the top tenth, would have added an additional 3 to 5 percentage points. Thus in 1952, for example, the top income-tenth actually accounted for at least 34 per cent of all personal income rather than 29 per cent.

The Kuznets Thesis: The Missing 95 Per Cent

Such phrases as "the remarkable equalization of income in the past twenty years," "the leveling out in the shares of national income by economic classes," and "one of the great social revolutions of history" rest largely on the statistics in Simon Kuznets' *Shares of Upper Income Groups in Income and Savings* (1953). The publishers, the otherwise impartial National Bureau of Economic Research, unprecedentedly claimed that the book showed the "United States has traveled a considerable distance toward absolute equality of incomes."[25] The study has decisively influenced most contemporary writings, by both scholars and popular writers, on the distribution of income in the United States. Its conclusions and assumptions have hardly been disputed.

In the strictest sense, the Kuznets book is a highly technical study of the tax returns of the 5 per cent of the population with the highest per-capita income. Kuznets' basic thesis is that, since 1939, the income-share of the top 1 per cent and the top 5 per cent of the population has dropped sharply and fairly consistently and that this decline is permanent. From 1939 to 1946, the income-share of the top 1 per cent declined 27 per cent, and the income-share of the top 5 per cent dropped 28 per cent. Excluding capital gains and before deducting Federal income taxes, the upper 1 per cent received 14.0 per cent of the income in 1919, 17.2 per cent in 1929, 12.3 per cent in 1941, and 9.6 per cent in 1946. The upper 5 per cent received 26.1 per cent of the income in 1919, 32.1 per cent in 1932, 25.7 per cent in 1941, and 20.0 per cent in 1946.[26]

Kuznets points out that between 1919 and 1938 the share of the upper 5 per cent declined an average of 0.4 per cent during periods of expansion in the business cycle, but rose an average of 1.5 per cent during recessions.[27] Although he shows that the percentage share of the upper 5 per cent climbed during the 1944–46 period of business prosperity, Kuznets predicted that it would fall again.

He believes that the decline of the upper 5 per cent is permanent because it reflects "far-reaching shifts in the industrial structure, employment opportunities, earning power of capital, and the tax system of the country."[28] Unfortunately, Kuznets gives only two pages (out of more than 700) to a consideration of these crucial factors, even though the validity of his work is largely contingent upon them.

The first factor Kuznets cites as proof of this permanent change is the rapid post-1939 rise in employment, during which the income-shares of the lower-income groups increased more rapidly than those of the higher-income groups. He assumes that periods of business contraction and unemployment, during which the income-shares of the top 5 per cent increase, will not be a major economic problem in the future. But four successively more severe recessions in the post-World War II period have demonstrated the fallacy of this premise.

Another proof, according to Kuznets, is the continuing growth in income of the farm population since 1939. But farm income—a highly variable factor, of course—has shown a fairly consistent decline since the peak year of 1948, both in share of national income and often in dollars per family. Adjusted for inflation, the 1958 total net income of the average farm family was only 15 per cent above the 1937–41 level, while income for the nation as a whole rose about three times the farm rate.

A third trend offered as evidence by Kuznets is the decline in importance of income from property in relation to the allegedly more equitably distributed income from salaries, wages, and entrepreneurial occupations. But there has been no such relative decline in corporate profits, and Kuznets has furthermore overlooked the significance of undistributed corporate profits. Nor is there any evidence that the distribution of wages and salaries is very equitable. In 1954, for example, the lowest income-fifth received 2.5 per cent of the national wage and salary income; the highest fifth, 44.7 per cent.[29]

Next Kuznets points to the experience of workers in finance, transportation, and communications between 1939 and 1948. He cites their disproportionately small increase in income, their decline as a percentage of the labor force, and the narrowing of the income gaps between these workers and those in manufacturing. But their disproportionately small income gains were due primarily to their higher employment in 1939. And the reduced differences in average income are a result of full employment since 1939.

Kuznets' fifth proof is the impact of taxation in lowering the income-share of the top 5 per cent. But, as we shall see in the next chapter, the effect of taxes on the highest incomes is commonly exaggerated.

Kuznets uses the Federal income-tax returns as his source of data. He measures income-size by dividing a return's total income by the number of persons covered by the return. The units with the greatest per-capita income are his base—and not the more significant consumer or spending units with the highest dollar incomes regardless of family size. This different base creates a substantially different result. Kuznets argues that he cannot use the family or spending unit because it may be represented by more than one tax return—although there is little likelihood of this in view of the tax advantages of joint returns and the small proportion of very high-income families with more than one earner. Or, he says, more than one spending unit may be covered by one tax return—but by definition a spending unit is made up of persons who pool their incomes and are financially one unit.[30]

As a result of this per-capita-income yardstick, Kuznets excludes from the economic elite many families who logically should be included. For example, according to Kuznets' theory, a family of two earning $20,000 a year is more prosperous than a family of five receiving $40,000. But a family of five saves through numerous economies, a point Kuznets concedes, and can attain the same standard of living on a substantially lower per-capita cost than a family of two. This built-in bias against large families is significant since the average high-income family is larger than the nation's average family—and particularly significant since World War II, when the high-income families have increased their size substantially.

Not too surprisingly, Kuznets' upper 5 per cent contains an extraordinarily large percentage of two-person families. In 1947 and 1948 they accounted for 22 per cent of the total population, but they comprised 64 per cent of Kuznets' sample.[31]

Since, despite these objections, the spending units and the Kuznets income-tax units pretty well coincide, it is clear that the one major difference in determining the top 5 per cent is the Kuznets procedure of dividing the income by the number of persons on the return. With this per-capita approach, a number of top-income families are replaced by families with an income that is smaller as a total, although greater per capita. Thus, his method produces a smaller total income and smaller income-share for the top 5 per cent.[32] And the disproportionate postwar increase in the size of wealthy families has served to produce a statistical decline in the income-share of his top 5 per cent.

The Office of Business Economics of the Department of Commerce, in a similar study, has computed data on the shares of the upper 5 per cent of consumer units. Its statistics are similar to Kuznets' in their failure to include most corporate income-in-kind, undeclared income, and undistributed profits, but differ in that the yardstick for the top 5 per cent is total income, not per-capita income. As a result, in many instances it allocates to the income-share of its upper 5 per cent of the population as much as an additional 2 percentage points. Kuznets claimed that in 1944 the upper 5 per cent received 18.7 per cent of the national income before taxes; the Department of Commerce figure was 20.7 per cent. Kuznets gave 20.0 per cent for 1946; the Department of Commerce 21.3 per cent. According to the Commerce figures, the income-share of the upper 5 per cent did not continue to decline after 1948, as Kuznets had predicted. Commerce statistics also indicate that the drop in the income-share of the richest 5 per cent *after taxes* was only about one-tenth in nearly all the post-World War II years.[33]

A more fundamental shortcoming in Kuznets' analysis is that he ignores the major factor of unreported income, which followed the inception of high tax rates, in 1941. It is surely no coincidence that the high tax rates and the decline in the before-taxes income-share of the top 5 per cent began in the same year. Yet Kuznets surprisingly assumes that under-reporting is "more prevalent and relatively more significant at lower income levels," although he offers no convincing data to prove the point.[34] As stated earlier in this chapter, much stronger evidence to the contrary exists in the tax audits. Kuznets, in addition, makes no adjustment for under-statement of tax-exempt income—for the purpose of concealing past or present money income—thereby overlooking an economic factor of considerable significance, since state and local government tax-free interest payments have increased sharply in recent years. Kuznets also fails to take into account corporate income-in-kind, in fact, any income-in-kind other than imputed rent.[35]

One of the most important weaknesses of Kuznets' study is his treatment of undistributed corporate profits, which have sharply increased in value since 1941. Since a good part of them will be realized as capital gains in the form of rising stock values, high dividends during periods of lower profits, and even direct distribution at some future time, they cannot be passed over lightly. Kuznets dispatched the problem very briefly by allocating an experimental, undisclosed percentage of the undistributed profits to the top 1 per cent and 5 per cent in 1939, 1944, and 1946.[36] He found that the 1939–46 disposable income-share of the top 1 per cent consequently dropped only 23 per cent, instead of the 36 per cent he obtained by ignoring undistributed profits. Allowing for a 25-per-cent reserve of profits by corporations and allocating a very conservative 70 per cent of the distributed profits to the top 5 per cent, Kuznets would have had to add more than 2 percentage points to the share of the upper 5 per cent in 1946 and more than 3 percentage points in 1947.[37] Thus, instead of 20 per cent of the income in 1946, the figure would have been 22 per cent.

If unreported money income and the various forms of nonsalary and nonmoney income—dividends, expense accounts, entrepreneurial income—are added to the income-share of the top 5 per cent, the Kuznets findings are significantly altered. Add to this the methodological limitations of Kuznets' technique, and his conclusions become even less plausible.

The study of the distribution of income has become vastly more complex since the New Deal, primarily because the forms and concepts of compensation for the top-income groups have changed in response to the increase in taxation rates since 1941. In large part, the seeming proof of increased income equality in the United States reflects a failure to appreciate the significance of the new circumstances. Instead of accepting the unverified assertions of basic changes in income distribution, let us first attempt to understand the complexities of the new ways of compensating the rich and the new means of tax avoidance.

2

Taxation and Inequality

It is widely believed that, as Ernest van den Haag and Ralph Ross put it, "the effect of progressive income taxes in diminishing the income of the upper brackets is too plain to need rehearsing."[1] But the impact of Federal income taxes on the actual distribution of wealth has been minimal, if not negligible. The desire to avoid the burden of high taxes has given rise to new factors in the distribution of wealth, which have so complicated the picture that a change in form has been mistaken by many for a basic change in content. A careful study of the topic will hardly sustain this illusion.

Contrary to common belief, heavy taxation of upper-income groups did not begin with the advent of the New Deal; it began only with the approach of United States involvement in World War II. Higher income taxation came as a response of the Roosevelt Administration to world events and not as a result of a conscious commitment to a social policy of reducing inequalities in the distribution of wealth.

As a matter of historical record, the New Deal was not seriously interested in taxation as a means of income equalization—despite its frequent assertions that it was. Roosevelt actively supported the Revenue Act of 1934, but his support for the somewhat stronger 1935 Act was equivocal and was finally obtained only because he feared the growing appeal of Huey Long's "Share-the-Wealth Clubs" and attacks by progressives in Congress. Even so, in a number of important

30

areas, the provisions of the two Acts were hardly designed to redistribute wealth effectively or reduce the capital accumulations of the rich. The estate-tax rates, which the 1932 Act set at 2 per cent for each bracket above $70,000, were raised to 3 per cent on amounts above $70,000 and up to $4.5 million, after which the rate dropped to 2 per cent. The corporate income tax was raised from 12 per cent to 15 per cent in 1936, to 19 per cent in 1939; not until 1942 was it raised to 40 per cent.[2]

Before 1941, the New Deal practice on personal-income taxation was, despite its difference in verbiage, essentially a continuation of that of the Hoover Administration. In 1929 and 1940, when the national personal income was almost the same, Federal receipts from personal income taxes were virtually identical—$1.323 billion in 1929 and $1.393 billion in 1940. But in 1941, the Federal personal income tax, increased because of the growing military budget, produced revenue one-half more than in 1940, although personal income increased only 14 per cent. In 1944, personal income was twice the 1940 level, but the tax yield was twelve times as great.[3] While much of this increased burden fell on the upper-income groups—enough to stimulate their search for new ways to avoid the highest tax brackets—the major weight fell on income groups that had never before been subjected to the income tax.

Thus, the ironic fact is that the extension of the income tax to middle- and low-income classes was the only original aspect of the New Deal tax policy.

Taxation: Theory and Practice

The feature of the income-tax structure that purportedly has had a major impact is the extremely steep tax rates (up to 91 per cent) on the very largest incomes. Actually, the resulting varied and ingenious methods of tax avoidance have substantially lessened the importance of these theoretically high rates.

Since 1941, members of the economic elite have attempted to receive their income in nontaxable forms or to postpone receiving it until retirement, when they will be in lower income brackets. There has been a strong downward shift in income-bracket levels, with an increasing proportion in the $25,000–$100,000 bracket, and in some years there has been an absolute drop in the number of returns reporting more than $100,000. More important, however, has been the trend away from the forms of income subject to high tax rates (salaries, wages, and certain types of property income) and toward tax-free interest, capital gains, and many other forms of income taxed at much lower rates or not at all. The proportionate importance of these forms of income to total income rises sharply in every income category over $10,000 a year.

Under Roosevelt, up to 1941, the actual, as opposed to the theoretical, tax rates on very high incomes were not very different from those under Herbert Hoover. Theoretically, the statutory tax is levied on straight income, none of which is derived from capital gains or other sources taxed at lower rates, from which no deductions are made, and no evasion attempted. In 1932, the highest possible tax rate on incomes of $1 million and up was 54 per cent, but only 47 per cent was actually collected. In 1938, the maximum theoretical tax rate had increased to 72 per cent, but only 44 per cent was collected. By 1957, the highest possible tax rate was 91 per cent, but only 52 per cent was collected.[4] As J. Keith Butters, Harvard economist, has written in his major study of taxation and the rich, *Effects of Taxation—Investment by Individuals* (1953), "By far the most striking and significant feature . . . is the large excess of theoretical over actual tax rates on upper bracket individuals when these rates are computed for income inclusive of all net capital gains."[5]

The income of the richest tenth is reduced less than 10 per cent by Federal income taxes. And, of course, the other tenths also show a net reduction in earnings after income taxes. Thus, it should come as no surprise that the distribution of income by tenths after Federal income taxes, shown in Table II, page 34, is practically the same as the distribution before taxes (see Table I, page 14). The slight changes in income-shares effected by the income tax have benefited income-tenths in the upper half almost as frequently as income-tenths in the lower half. These fundamental facts have been ignored by those who interpret the tax system on the basis of their arbitrary preconceptions rather than on the basis of its actual effects.

THE REVOLUTION IN TAXATION

Now we see that progressive taxation of incomes has not been applied to the economic elite sufficiently to change the distribution of income-shares, and that although the economic elite has been subject to heavier Federal income taxation since 1941, the same factor that stimulated a higher tax rate on the rich also produced, for the first time in American history, permanent and significant income taxation of low- and middle-income earners.

In 1939, only 4.0 million families or persons were subject to Federal income taxation; in 1940, 7.5 million; in 1941, 17.6 million; in 1944, 42.4 million; and in 1957, 46.9 million.[6] Similarly, the share of the national personal income subject to Federal income taxes was 10 per cent in 1939, 24 per cent in 1941, and 43 per cent in 1957.[7] The net effect, since there was a fairly stable distribution of income over that period, was to tax lower- and middle-income classes that had never been taxed before. This was done by reducing the minimum tax exemption and extending the tax scale. In 1957, 66 per cent of all reported incomes were taxed at the base rate of

TABLE II

PERCENTAGE OF NATIONAL PERSONAL INCOME RECEIVED BY EACH INCOME-TENTH AFTER FEDERAL INCOME TAXES

	Highest	2nd	3rd	4th	5th	6th	7th	8th	9th	Lowest
1947	31 (−2)*	15	12	10	9	8 (+1)	6	5 (+1)	3	1
1949	28 (−2)	15	13 (+1)	11	9	8	7 (+1)	5	3	1
1950	27 (−2)	15	13	11	10 (+1)	8	7 (+1)	5	3	1
1951	28 (−3)	15	13 (+1)	11 (+1)	9	8	7 (+1)	5	3	1
1952	27 (−3)	15	13 (+1)	11	10 (+1)	8	7 (+1)	5	3	1
1953	28 (−3)	15	12	11 (+1)	9	8	7 (+1)	5	4 (+1)	1
1954	27 (−2)	15	13	11	9	8	7 (+1)	5	4 (+1)	1
1955	27 (−2)	16	13	11	10 (+1)	8	6	5 (+1)	3	1

* Numbers in parentheses indicate change in percentage points from before-tax income.

Source: Bureau of the Census, *Statistical Abstract of the United States—1957* (Washington, D.C.: Government Printing Office, 1957), p. 309. These data, collected by the Survey Research Center, include capital gains but exclude income-in-kind.

20 per cent. For married couples, taxable income began at $3,500 in 1929, $2,500 in 1935 and 1936, $1,500 in 1941, $1,000 in 1944, and $1,200 from 1948 on. Inflation sharply increased this trend by reducing the value of both incomes and exemptions, and its influence continues. The percentage of Federal revenue yielded by personal-income taxes increased from a scant 9 per cent in 1916 to 18 per cent in 1941, 41 per cent in 1946, and 53 per cent in 1960. At the same time, the percentage of Federal revenue yielded by corporate-profits taxes grew from 8 per cent in 1916 to 26 per cent in 1941, and 30 per cent in 1946, and fell to 28 per cent in 1960.[8]

In this process of incorporating more and more of the American population into the Federal income tax system, a moderate degree of progressive taxation has been maintained. The income tax is practically the only major tax that is not basically regressive. Nevertheless, the income tax paid by the average family in the lowest income-fifth—in 1957, amounting to 3.3 per cent of their income—constitutes a greater hardship for those living on an emergency budget than does the tax burden of 13.7 per cent paid in the same year by the average family in the richest income-fifth.[9]

The basic tax rate on taxable income (i.e., income after all deductions for dependents, charitable donations, medical expenses, etc.) begins at 20 per cent. A major proportion of legitimate expenses is unclaimed annually, and most of this can, we know, be attributed to low- and middle-income families.[10] Fewer than 10 per cent of those earning less than $2,000 take credit for deductible expenditures beyond their dependents and the flat 10 per cent allowed on the short form.[11] This failure is due in large part to the complexity of filling out a "long form" for deductions. Deductions, it should be pointed out, must be quite high before they will save a family anything. For example, a family that can claim no deductions for interest, state taxes, donations, casualty losses, or the like must have medical expenses amounting to at least 13 per cent of its total income before it will save anything.

Joint-filing provisions for husbands and wives, intended to lower their tax burden, were of no benefit in 70 per cent of the joint returns filed in 1957, which were from low- and middle-income groups.[12] In the upper-income brackets, however, the joint return can be of enormous benefit. On an income of $35,000, it can realize a peak saving of 40 per cent of the tax bill.[13]

The Combined Impact of All Taxes

Most recent commentators who have credited the Federal income tax with redistributing income have ignored the fact that it is only one of a number of taxes—and the only one that is in some measure progressive. Therefore, any discussion of distribution of income after taxes must consider the consequences of all taxes.

In general, local and states taxes are regressive. More than half—59 per cent in 1958—of all state tax revenues come from sales taxes. About one-half of the expenditures of an average spending unit earning a cash income of less than $1,000 a year are subject to general sales or excise taxes, but only one-third of the expenditures of those earning $10,000-plus are so taxed.[14] In effect, corporations present the public with additional hidden taxes. The corporation income tax is, as the *Wall Street Journal* puts it, "treated by the corporations as merely another cost which they can pass on to their customers."[15] It has been variously estimated that one-third to one-half of this tax is shifted to the consumers. Furthermore, at least two-thirds of American corporations add all payroll-tax costs to their prices.[16]

The Tax Foundation has calculated actual taxes paid as a percentage of income for all income classes in 1958 (see Table III, page 37). Its figures show that state and local taxes are

TABLE III

PERCENTAGE OF 1958 TOTAL INCOME PAID IN FEDERAL, STATE,
AND LOCAL TAXES,* BY INCOME CLASS

Income Class (In dollars)	Share of Taxes (In per cent)		
	Federal	State and Local	Total†
0– 2,000	9.6	11.3	21.0
2,000– 4,000	11.0	9.4	20.4
4,000– 6,000	12.1	8.5	20.6
6,000– 8,000	13.9	7.7	21.6
8,000–10,000	13.4	7.2	20.6
10,000–15,000	15.1	6.5	21.6
15,000–plus	28.6	5.9	34.4
Average	16.1	7.5	23.7

* Social-insurance taxes are not included.
† Because of rounding, items do not always add up to totals.

Source: Tax Foundation, *Allocation of the Tax Burden by Income Class* (New York: Tax Foundation, 1960), p. 17.

regressive, and that all Federal taxes combined, although tending to be progressive, fall much more substantially on the low-income classes than is generally realized. Included in its calculations are all local, state, and Federal personal-income taxes; inheritance, estate, and gift taxes; corporate-profit taxes (it assumes that one-half of this is shifted to the public); excise and sales taxes; customs and property taxes. Excluded are the highly regressive social-insurance taxes, which take 7.3 per cent of the total income of those earning $2,000 or less but only 1.5 per cent in the $15,000-plus class.

These Tax Foundation data indicate that the combined American tax system is scarcely "progressive" and hardly in accord with the image of it nourished by most social scientists and students of contemporary America.[17] If, despite innumerable loopholes, the Federal income tax has introduced a moderately progressive but greatly misunderstood and overemphasized taxation, the Federal excise and customs—and most major local and state—taxes have seriously lessened its impact. The income tax paid by the lower-income classes is, for the most part, money that would otherwise go for essential personal and family needs; in this light, the tax burden is substantially heavier for the lower-income classes than for the higher-income classes.

WELFARE AND INCOME INEQUALITY

Theoretically, it would be possible for the revenues from regressive taxation to be directed to welfare expenditures for lower-income groups, and for the inequality of income distribution to be reduced thereby to a significant extent. This has actually been achieved, in the eyes of a number of proponents of the income-redistribution thesis. "Through a combination of patchwork revisions of the system—tax laws, minimum wage laws, subsidies and guarantees and regulations of various sorts, plus labor union pressures and new management attitudes—we had repealed the Iron Law of Wages," wrote Frederick Lewis Allen in *The Big Change*. "We had brought about a virtually automatic redistribution of income from the well-to-do to the less well-to-do."[18] The plausibility of this thesis has only been strengthened by the attacks of conservatives on the alleged "welfare state" created by the Roosevelt Administration.

However, this viewpoint is not sustained by a careful examination of the motives for the revisions in the tax structure: The reason for high taxation, at least since 1933, has been not to redistribute income but to pay for extraordinary costs—primarily military from 1940 on—in the most expeditious way. We have not taxed the rich to give to the poor; we have taxed both the rich and the poor and, at least since 1940, contributed only a small fraction of the proceeds to the welfare of the poor.

Consider, for example, 1958. In that year, Federal revenue from personal-income, estate and gift, corporate-profit, and excise and customs taxes, excluding the self-financing social-insurance program, amounted to $69 billion.[19] The families and unattached individuals in the $0–$2,000 class contributed $1.066 billion, those in the $2,000–$4,000 class contributed $4.971 billion. But the Federal government spent only $4.509 billion on what by the most generous definition may be called "welfare." Included were all expenditures for public assistance, public health, education, and "other welfare," and half of the outlay for farm parity prices and income, and public housing. In 1949, Federal expenditures for welfare were $2.037 billion; in 1954, they were $2.451 billion, and in 1955, $4.062 billion. In each of these years, however, the total Federal tax payments of the spending units earning less than $4,000 were greater than these welfare expenditures. If all Federal welfare expenditures went to the $0–$4,000 class—which was certainly not the case—this class more than paid for them.

In brief, welfare spending has not changed the nature of income inequality, nor raised the standard of living of the lowest-income classes above what it would have reached if they had not been subjected to Federal taxation. It might be claimed that these classes must assume some responsibility for the nation's "larger obligations," but this is not an argument advanced by those who assert that we have redistributed income through taxation and welfare measures.

MEANS OF TAX AVOIDANCE

The most effective way of avoiding taxes, of course, is by not declaring one's income. In 1957, 9 per cent of the national personal income—$28 billion—never appeared in tax returns. As indicated in Chapter 1, most of this $28 billion was received by the upper-income class. This problem of undeclared income was negligible before 1941, but, as an Internal Revenue official suggested in 1959, "When the tax rates were low, there wasn't much to be gained." The strictly legal loopholes for tax avoidance are numerous. Still, as one tax accountant put it, "Taxpayers in the 50% bracket or higher start getting a feeling of anger . . . and they start looking for ways to lighten the load. First they take the legal steps of tax avoidance. But many find this doesn't give them enough relief."[20] The wide extent of tax evasion makes it obvious that the risks involved are insufficient to discourage the practice.

Capital gains are the single most important means of avoiding the theoretically high tax on large incomes. The highest tax rate on capital gains—profits from sales of stock, property, etc., that have been held longer than six months—is only 25 per cent. It is significant that in 1942, soon after the income-tax burden on the highest-income groups was increased, Congress reduced this holding period from two years to six months. The effect was to offset the increased tax burden on one form of wealth by reducing it on another. The act was based on the specious assumption that the flow of profits on stocks and sales was "long-term" windfall profit rather than income. In 1957, 20 per cent of the total income of the $100,000-plus class was in capital gains, and this income was, at the most, taxed at a rate only slightly higher than the rate on the taxable income of the lowest-income classes. By way of contrast, only three-tenths of 1 per cent of the total income of those in the $3,500–$4,000 class originated as capital gains that year.[21]

As a result of the preferred tax status of capital gains, the wealthy have attempted to maximize the means for obtaining them, and the concept of executives' compensation in the corporation has been accordingly adjusted. "You can't compete for executive talent today without a gimmick," declared David Sarnoff, Chairman of the Radio Corporation of America, several years ago.[22] These gimmicks take innumerable forms—deferred-compensation plans, profit-sharing trusts, stock options, and the like—but all have two common purposes: to maximize the amount of income going to executives as capital gains and to postpone disbursement of part of their income until retirement, when most will fall into lower-income categories. Before 1940, about 700 companies had such plans in operation; by 1946, 9,000 firms had them.[23]

Under a deferred-compensation plan, the executive receives, after retirement, his own payments to the plan as tax-free income; he pays only a capital-gains tax on the company's contributions. These plans differ in detail but not in essential form. For top executives, special arrangements are often made. Harley J. Earl, a General Motors vice-president who retired in December, 1958, after having earned a peak salary of $130,000 a year, receives $50,000 a year until December, 1963, and $75,000 a year for the ten years thereafter.[24] Although not always so generous, most companies, especially if they are closely owned, sponsor similar plans for top executives.

The stock option, a tax-avoidance factor of tremendous importance to corporate executives, was introduced in the 1950 Revenue Act, and it has become a major means of compensating members of the economic elite. By 1957, 77 per cent of the largest manufacturing corporations had set up option plans. Under the terms of the Act, an option on a company's stock is offered to an executive at no less than 85 per cent (in practice, it is generally 95 per cent) of the current market value. The executive must wait at least eighteen months before he exercises the option—if he chooses to exercise it. If the market price rises, as it almost invariably does in an inflationary economy, the executive buys the stock at its original low price; then, if he waits six months to sell, he pays only the capital-gains tax on the profit. If the stock's price falls 20 per cent or more below the option price, the option price can again be reduced to 95 per cent of the average market price for the twelve months preceding the new change.

"In the past five years," *U.S. News & World Report* observed in 1955, "these options have produced a whole new crop of millionaires." One aircraft company gave thirteen executives an option on 30,000 shares in 1951; in 1955, they realized a 370 per cent profit. A rubber company granted a vice-president an option on 10,000 shares worth $213,800 in 1951; in 1955, they were worth $547,000. In 1957, Frank Pace, Jr., and John J. Hopkins exercised their options to buy General Dynamics stock then valued at $1,125,000 and $1,220,000, respectively; their option price was about one-third the market value at the time of the stock sale. In January, 1956, Donald W. Douglas, Sr., of Douglas Aircraft, exercised an option for 15,000 shares at $16.50 each at a time when the market price had risen to $86—a profit of more than $1 million. During 1956, when executives at Pittsburgh Plate Glass purchased 40,000 company shares at an option price of $41, the market price ranged from $74 to $96. Beginning in 1951, U.S. Steel granted its executives stock options with a face value of $49 million; on August 8, 1957, the stocks were worth $133 million on the market.[25]

Those in the high income-tax bracket find it profitable to receive part of their income in totally tax-exempt interest. In 1957, they received almost $600 million of income in this form. Kuznets, in his study of the top 5 per cent, did not allocate any of this nontaxable income to this income group after 1940. However, we know that the economic elite have been rapidly increasing their tax-exempt holdings since 1929 and that they now own almost all available holdings of this type.[26] We also know that the sales and yield of tax-free state and local securities have risen very sharply since 1939. Thus we can see the rising importance of tax-free income to the wealthy. These securities yield as high as 6 per cent, although the 1959 average yield on high-grade municipal bonds was 4.0 per cent. With a taxable income of $70,000 to $80,000, a tax-free return of 4.0 per cent is equal to a taxable 21.0 per cent return after taxes. In the $150,000–$200,000 bracket, a tax-free 4.0 per cent return is equal to a taxable 40 per cent after taxes, and a tax-free 5.25 per cent is equal to a taxable 52.5 per cent after taxes.

Contrary to common opinion, inherited wealth and large capital accumulations have not been seriously affected by the existing tax laws. Here the legal escape clauses are so numerous that the impact of the high estate tax—theoretically up to 77 per cent on $10 million—is, in actuality, nominal. In 1951, the total net value of estates reported on taxable returns was taxed at only 14 per cent.[27]

A married man can divide his estate so that one-half is taxed at his death and one-half at his wife's death, thereby sharply lowering the tax bracket. In this way alone, the taxes on a $300,000 estate would be reduced from $62,700 to $17,900, and the taxes on $10,060,000 estate from slightly more than $6 million to less than $2.5 million.[28]

However, two major alternatives—gifts and trusts—allows persons with taxable estates of $100,000 and up to avoid the heaviest rates. Gifts made by wealthy individuals during their lifetime are taxed much less than the same gifts made as bequests after their death. The gift-tax rate on $1 million is 27.75 per cent; the inheritance-tax rate is 31.4 per cent. But even this rate is often avoided. A man may split up his estate by giving $6,000 a year to his wife and $3,000 a year—or $6,000, if his wife agrees—to as many other persons as he wishes. Only the donor is taxed on the gift at the gift-tax rate, which begins at 2.25 per cent under $5,000. In addition, a $60,000 basic lifetime exemption is allowed every couple.

By 1951, about 45 per cent of the value of estates worth more than $500,000 had been placed in trusts.[29] The trust guarantees that estate taxes will not be paid by a family on the amount set aside for at least two generations after the death of its founder. It divides the family fortune, for purposes of taxation, into smaller units and can result, under the 1952 tax laws, in tax savings as high as 70 per cent on the income of property placed in trust. By September, 1959, all the states had enacted "custodian laws" to allow members of families to organize and manage trusts in the name of minors, permitting the eventual avoidance of estate taxes, division of income for current tax purposes, and elimination of cumbersome legal procedures for the organization of trusts.

Since the 1952 tax law, a rapidly growing number of special provisions have been created that apply to relatively small groups among the wealthy but add up to a cumulative trend toward legal tax avoidance. The fantastic complexity of the tax law has not succeeded in dimming the sheer genius of tax lawyers, who have aided the economic elite to circumscribe, in a perfectly legal manner, many of the more onerous tax provisions. Their ultimate success, however, can be attributed neither to their ingenuity nor to the intricacy of the tax law; it results from the failure of political administrations over the past four decades to enact tax legislation that seriously challenges the economic power of the wealthy. All recent Administration suggestions for closing these tax loopholes have been coupled with proposals to lower the tax rates on the richest income classes—thereby leaving the wealthy in substantially their present economic position.

Viewing this sharp contrast between the avowed equalitarian sentiments of most politicians and the legal and economic reality of the tax structure, Stanley S. Surrey, of the Harvard Law School, has rightly concluded that "the average congressman does not basically believe in the present rates of income tax in the upper brackets. When he sees them applied to individual cases, he thinks them too high and therefore unfair. . . . Since they are not, however, willing to reduce those rates directly, the natural outcome is indirect reduction through special provisions."[30]

The complexity of the effect of taxation should not be allowed to obscure the basic trends—the growing tax burden on the low- and middle-income classes, and the huge disparity between theoretical and actual tax rates for the wealthy. The conclusion is inescapable: Taxation has not mitigated the fundamentally unequal distribution of income. If anything it has perpetuated inequality by heavily taxing the low- and middle-income groups—those least able to bear its burden.

3

The Distribution of Wealth

The pattern of inequality that we have seen in the distribution of income also prevails in the larger picture—the distribution of stock, real estate, savings, and all other forms of wealth. Once again, we find the heavy concentration of holdings at the top, the thin scattering at the bottom.

The arresting fact is that, as of 1953, the 9 per cent at the top of the income groupings owned more than 46 per cent of the nation's net private assets. And, in that same year, the wealthiest 11 per cent of spending units—those having a net worth of $25,000 and up—owned 60 per cent of the private assets, according to the Survey Research Center. Half of this wealthiest 11 per cent were also members of the income class earning over $7,500—a fraction that would be larger if there were not so many farmers included in the wealthiest asset group. (Farmers are not actually comparable to other wealthy spending units because of the latter's much larger and more profitable net worth in business and investment assets.)[1]

And so it is evident that a tiny minority of the American people possess both the highest income and the greatest share of private assets.

SAVINGS

Savings are a major instrument of economic power. They are distributed much more inequitably among the income-tenths than annual personal income, and this inequality has not been lessened with rising dollar and real incomes for the lower tenths. This is a logical result of the necessity for the lower-income segments to spend all their incomes—or more— to obtain the basic essentials of life. In each postwar year, one-third of all families and unattached individuals have been spending more than they earn. The red-ink proportion for 1950, as an example, ranged from 36 per cent in the $0–$3,000 class to 13 per cent in the $7,500-plus class.[2] And even though lower- and middle-income spending units may save at some time, by the end of their earning career, they generally have accumulated very little. The expenses of raising a family and then retirement soon dissipate their savings.

There can be little dispute over which income classes have the highest savings-to-income ratio. Clearly, the higher the income the greater the savings.

The distribution of net savings by income-tenths (see Table IV) shows the impact of low income and debt. Except for 1945, when there was a backlog of unspent war wages and a scarcity of goods to purchase, the highest income-tenth has owned the bulk of savings since at least 1929. The ability to save demonstrated by this group, and especially a small elite within it, has not been reduced by so-called progressive tax laws or a purported income redistribution.[3]

Liquid assets—such as checking and savings accounts, shares in savings-and-loan associations and credit unions, and government savings bonds—are of decisive importance to low- and even middle-income families exposed to layoffs, unemployment, or medical and other emergencies. Often they represent the entire margin between security and the relief rolls.

However, since the end of World War II, an average of at least one-quarter of American families and unattached individuals have had no liquid assets whatsoever. In early 1960,

TABLE IV

PERCENTAGE OF TOTAL NATIONAL NET SAVINGS OWNED BY EACH INCOME-TENTH

	1929	1935–36	1941	1945	1946	1947	1948	1949	1950
Highest	86	105	73	46	63	77	78	105	73
2nd	12	13	15	18	16	16	19	26	20
3rd	7	6	6	13	14	6	15	13	11
4th	5	2	5	8	7	6	6	8	10
5th	3	−1	5	5	4	3	6	1	4
6th	1	−2	3	4	1	4	2	*	−1
7th	*	−3	1	3	2	2	−1	−4	1
8th	0	−5	−1	3	1	−1	−3	−8	*
9th	−1	−5	−3	2	−3	−2	−5	−6	−2
Lowest	−13	−9	−4	−2	−5	−11	−17	−35	−16

* Less than one-half of 1 per cent.

Source: Data for 1929 are from Maurice Leven *et al., America's Capacity to Consume* (Washington, D.C.: Brookings Institution, 1934), p. 96; data for 1935–36, from National Resources Committee, *Consumer Expenditures in the United States* (Washington, D.C.: Government Printing Office, 1939), p. 51; data for 1941–50, from *Federal Reserve Bulletin,* August 1948, p. 923; September, 1951, p. 1067. Data for years after 1950 were never calculated. Because 1929 data exclude net savings for unattached individuals, concentration at the highest levels is slightly exaggerated.

for example, 24 per cent of the spending units had no liquid assets, 27 per cent had $1 to $500, and 63 per cent had less than $1,000.[4] Because the almost identical distribution existed in 1948, when money was worth more, there obviously has been an absolute decline in the financial security of Americans.

What are the correlations to this inability to save? By income: In early 1960, 52 per cent of those in the poorest income-fifth had no liquid assets, as compared to 6 per cent in the richest fifth. By age: In virtually any year, the greatest assets were found among spending units headed by persons aged fifty-five to sixty-four; the lowest assets were found among the group needing them most, the spending units headed by persons aged sixty-five years and over.[5] By occupation: In 1960, no liquid assets were held by 51 per cent of the spending units headed by unskilled or service workers, 28 per cent of the semiskilled, and 19 per cent of the skilled —as compared to 3 per cent of the professionals.[6]

Since World War II, one-tenth of the nation has owned an average of two-thirds of all liquid assets. But liquid assets are important to the low- and middle-income classes, since they provide economic security in an insecure economy. But they are not attractive to the wealthy, who have no need to pursue security and instead are seeking profit. The wealthy, it should be remembered, put only a small proportion of their savings into liquid assets. Nevertheless, since 1950 the top income-tenth has owned more than 36 per cent of all liquid assets—roughly the same percentage as their share of the nation's total private income.[7]

Historical data on savings patterns strongly indicate that this concentration was not diminished by the New Deal. This is not a very controversial assertion among specialists on savings, for as one of them, Raymond W. Goldsmith, put it, "it is fairly clear . . . that the upper-income groups have always accounted for the major part of total personal savings. . . . This fact, of course, has been known from all investigations made of the distribution of saving."[8]

STOCK OWNERSHIP

Almost all the theorists who contend there has been a redistribution of wealth in America concentrate their attention on one form of assets—stock shares in corporations. In a characteristic statement, Ernest van den Haag writes: "Corporate ownership is no longer confined to the upper classes. An increasing proportion of industry, of the productive wealth of the country, is owned by the middle- and lower-income brackets. Their money is becoming indispensable for investment, because the rich no longer can save enough to provide for all the investment needs of the economy. This shift in the ownership of wealth may be described as a peaceful, but not slow, process of socialization of the means of production."[9]

This idea of "people's capitalism"—the official and highly publicized concept of the New York Stock Exchange and the Advertising Council—is shared by too many social scientists who should know better. Popular economists, such as Adolf A. Berle, Jr., and Peter F. Drucker, have suggested that stock ownership has become very widely diffused and that there are no longer any sizable concentrations of stock held among individuals.[10] In reality, stock ownership, like every other form of wealth and assets, is very highly concentrated. This conclusion is supported by every reliable study of stock distribution in the United States.

The fact is that the concentration of stock ownership has shown no appreciable change since 1929. In that year, 51,000 individuals received one-half the value of the cash dividends received by all individual shareowners; in 1933 and 1937, this number was 45,000 and 61,000, respectively.[11] Also, in 1937, some 6.6 per cent of the population owned stock; this figure dropped to 5.1 per cent in 1956, and not until 1959 had it increased to 7.9 per cent.

Within the already small minority of the population owning stock, a very small percentage has always controlled the bulk of the stock, no matter how large the total number of stockholders. The Temporary National Economic Committee studied the distribution of shares among the 8.5 million individuals owning stock in 1,710 major companies in 1937–39. It found that 4.0 per cent of the owners of common stock held 64.9 per cent of it, and 4.5 per cent of the owners of preferred stock held 54.8 per cent of it.[12]

The Brookings Institution, in a study of 1951 stock ownership in 2,991 major corporations, discovered that only 2.1 per cent of the common-stock shareholdings owned 58 per cent of the common stock and that 1.1 per cent of the preferred stockholdings owned 46 per cent of the preferred stock. Thirty-one per cent of the common-stock shareholdings owned 32 per cent of the shares, and two-thirds of the common-stock shareholdings accounted for a mere one-tenth of the shares.[13] J. Keith Butters, in *Effects of Taxation—Investment by Individuals* (1953), estimates that in 1949, the spending units owning $100,000 or more in marketable stocks—who made up about one-fifth of 1 per cent of the total national spending units and 2 per cent of the stockholders—owned between 65 and 71 per cent of all the marketable stock held by individuals.[14]

These data unavoidably understate the concentration of stocks held by the wealthy few, for 36 per cent of the total stock in 1937, and 33 per cent in 1951, was owned by fiduciaries, foundations, etc., and these nonindividual shares are excluded from the stock distributions given above.[15] However, even though these holdings are not listed by individuals, they remain largely controlled by top-bracket stockholders primarily interested in devising means for avoiding various taxes.

TABLE V

THE DISTRIBUTION OF COMMON STOCK IN PUBLICLY OWNED
CORPORATIONS IN 1951

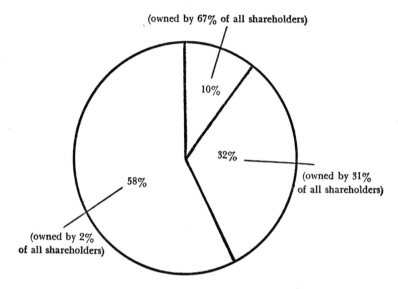

Source: Lewis H. Kimmel, *Share Ownership in the United States* (Washington, D.C.: Brookings Institution, 1952), pp. 43, 46.

As might be predicted, stock ownership is very inequitably distributed among the various income classes. In early 1959, only 14 per cent of the nation's spending units owned stock; ownership ranged from 6 per cent in the $5,000-or-less income class to 55 per cent in the $15,000-or-more income class. The $10,000-plus income class accounted for more than half the stockholders and owned about 75 per cent of the stock in 1949 and more than 80 per cent in early 1952. In 1959, it accounted for nine-tenths of those with holdings of $25,000 and up.[16]

Despite such conclusive data on stock-ownership concentration, the public has been subjected to a widespread advertising campaign alleging that the American corporation is owned democratically. They are told that the increase in the number of shareholders, from 6.5 million in 1952 to 12.5 million in 1959, is significant, even though there were 9 to 11 million stockholders in the smaller population of 1930. The annual stockholders' meeting is portrayed as a "town meeting," the epitome of democracy—despite the irony of a town meeting in which a few participants have most of the votes. Ignored is the fact that a growing number of these affairs are stage-managed by public-relations counselors, who are prepared for all contingencies. The conclusion is inevitable that there is little "people's" in "people's capitalism."[17]

"People's capitalism" has drawn into the market persons ignorant of basic economics, many of whom have lost on their investments and have made the stock market more unstable during short-term political developments. Too many of these persons do little more than outright gambling in stocks. As a result, the Securities and Exchange Commission has been attempting since 1956 to curb the small but growing number of brokers seeking to sell nearly worthless securities to the public. Indeed, the only group consistently benefiting from the strong element of speculative mania in "people's capitalism" has been the brokers. In 1959, brokerage firms opened 203 new branch offices, compared to 73 the year before, and dozens of them moved into what the *Wall Street Journal* described as "bigger, plushier New York offices."[18]

It is suggested that the supposedly growing ownership of stocks by worker pension funds and investment companies has made 50 million Americans indirect owners in the corporate structure, and that the proportionate returns of corporate profits to these Americans will rise as the holdings of pension and similar funds rapidly increase. "The corporate system," wrote Adolf A. Berle, Jr., in 1959, "is thus in effect operating to 'socialize' American industry but without intervention of the political state."[19] Because pension funds and insurance companies supplied 10 to 15 per cent of the industrial capital during the 1950's and are expected to supply even more throughout the 1960's, Berle foresaw the possibility of the managers of these funds achieving working control over the corporate structure.

However, this theory has a basic flaw. The trustees of these pension funds are not union officials, but, as Berle admits, primarily New York banks. These banks rarely vote their pension stockholdings, and they almost never oppose existing managerial control, since in most instances the employer has the right to transfer the pension account to another bank.

In nine out of ten instances, these funds buy no stock in their own corporation, and only occasionally have the total shares held by all pension funds amounted to more than 3 per cent of the outstanding stock of any company. The pension funds are, in fact, a very long way from achieving control of the corporate system. At the end of 1959, the pension funds owned a mere 3.5 per cent of all outstanding stock listed on the New York Stock Exchange.[20] Robert Tilove, a pension-fund consultant, predicts in *Pension Funds and Economic Freedom* (1959) that by 1965, they will own no more than 6.5 per cent. As more insured workers retire, the assets of the pension funds will decline, and by 1970, their holdings will probably have become even more inconsequential.[21]

Investment companies, which owned 5.8 per cent of the stock in 1959, are too limited by law to intimidate the corporations. Anyhow, they are hardly a force for democracy, since they are owned little more equitably than private stock.

We can only conclude that there has been an enormous exaggeration of the "socializing" effect of these institutions on the American corporation. Clearly, our only realistic yardstick for measuring the extent of democracy in corporate stockholding is the distribution of private ownership.

4

The Concentration of Corporate Power

The distribution of power over corporations, the dominant sector of the economy, is of major consequence in determining the extent to which America has attained a democratic economic structure.

Most recent theoretical discussions of the role of the corporation in American life have ignored the facts about the actual distribution of corporate power in favor of theories about the relationship of the corporation to the rest of society and the nature of the corporate executive as an individual.

The dominant image of the corporate leadership today is that of the responsible trustee. This concept has its roots in a basic proposition set forth by Berle and Gardiner Means as long ago as 1932, in *The Modern Corporation and Private Property*. They contended that stock ownership had been widely dispersed and that corporate management had been separated from stock ownership and from stock owners and now operated independently of the profit motive.

Although it is granted by practically all that corporate power is still very great, current theory suggests that it is self-restrained and socially responsible, a power in equilibrium with the state and the labor union. For many, it is an article of faith that its potential for social harm will not and could not be exercised.

There is a notion that corporate power is held in trust for the community. The corporate leadership, writes David Riesman in *The Lonely Crowd,* is "coming more and more to think of themselves as trustees for their beneficiaries."[1] The corporation, writes Berle, "has been compelled to assume in appreciable part the role of conscience-carrier of twentieth-century American society."[2] Further, he says, "the corporation is now, essentially, a nonstatist political institution, and its directors are in the same boat with public officeholders."[3]

Such assertions assume that the power of the stockholder is no longer a factor of major significance. They further assume that the corporate leadership has no interests that are in conflict with the "public's"—and that it shares none with the amorphous and presumably constantly expanding ranks of stockholders. In this view, the operating executives—the men who make the short- and intermediate-range decisions for the large corporations—have displaced the directors as architects of fundamental, long-range policies. "Corporate control," writes David E. Lilienthal, "far from being a virtual absolute in the majority of directors or stockholders, is now divided and diffused."[4] And so, it is suggested, the corporate managers, freed from responsibility to those whose only incentive is profit, have brought new motives to business leadership.

But the real question, the heart of the matter, is whether there is in fact a small group of persons in a position to exercise control over the corporate structure. If there is such a group, the matter of whether they actually utilize this power is secondary—the overriding consideration is, Do they have such power? It doesn't matter how they exercise this power, whether for their particular interests or for those of society as a whole. The philosophy of their views may be debatable; the anatomy of their power is not.

The facts, in brief, are these: In 1955 the 200 top non-financial companies—most of which dominated their respective industries as price and policy leaders—directly owned 43.0 per cent of the total assets of 435,000 nonfinancial corporations; this amounted to at least 18.3 per cent of the total national reproducible tangible assets of $891 billion.[5]

These corporations were controlled by approximately 2,500 men—and probably even fewer.

These men, in both direct ownership of economic assets and control over the corporate structure, are the most important single group in the American economic elite.

INTERLOCKING DIRECTORATES

Interlocking directorates, whereby a director of one corporation also sits on the board of one or more other corporations, are a key device for concentrating corporate power, since they enable one corporation to wield influence over one or more others. The director representing Company A can, by sitting on the board of Company B, exert influence over it to increase its financial cooperation with Company A or make purchases from it. He can also act to prevent Company B from manufacturing a competing product or diversifying into a field occupied by Company A.

The Temporary National Economic Committee discovered that in 1939, within the top 200 corporations, there were 3,511 directorships held by about 2,500 persons.[6] Offhand, this would seem to suggest that interlocking directorships were not very significant.

But let us look at corporations that rank below the top 200 in size. It is, after all, much more likely that a giant corporation would attempt to influence a corporation smaller than itself than one larger or the same size. When one tabulates the number of directorships in corporations of every size held by the directors of the top 200 corporations, a pattern of extensive interlocking directorships emerges, involving a very large percentage of the top directors. Here, then, is the dominant fact of economic control: the top 200 corporations cooperate with each other and exert influence within innumerable smaller companies. Generally, of course, the larger corporation sends its representative to the board of the smaller firm.

In 1957, Sidney J. Weinberg, of the investment house of Goldman, Sachs, sat on not only five boards among the top 200 corporations, but six boards of smaller companies; T. W. Collins, an officer-director of Crown-Zellerbach, was on seven boards below the top 200; and James Bruce, a director of National Dairy, sat on three boards among the top 200 and 13 lesser ones.

Interlocking directorates are classified by the Federal Trade Commission into seven major forms:

1. Between competing firms—whether direct (one company's director sits on another company's board) or indirect (two companies share a director whose primary tie is with a third company)—and thereby control or eliminate competition. In 1946, five of the 12 big meat packers were indirectly interlocked, 16 of the 23 largest sugar companies were directly and indirectly interlocked, and 17 of the 20 largest petroleum companies were interlocked.[7]

2. Between companies in related industries that are interested in preventing diversification into directly competitive products. Such interlocking exists in the glass industry, for example, so that bottle and sheet-glass makers will not encroach on each other.

3. Between companies in a single industry that face similar problems and share a community of interests, whether direct or indirect. Thus, the four largest electrical-machinery corporations were indirectly interlocked in 1946.

4. Between purchasing company and supplier, whose relationship generally involves a strategic advantage to the purchasing company. The food industry is heavily interlocked with the container industry, the automobile companies with

the parts manufacturers. This is the most important form of interlocking.

5. Between producer and distributor, for the purpose of gaining preferential markets. Thus Westinghouse Air Brake Company is linked with most of the major manufacturers of railroad cars and locomotives, and the glass-making companies with the distilleries and drug companies.

6. Between corporation and financial institution, to provide adequate credit for the corporation and possible denial of credit to competitors. Myriad examples of this exist.

7. Between companies with common ownership. The General Motors–Du Pont–U.S. Rubber–Ethyl group is an excellent case in point.

The annual proxy statement rarely gives details of a company's contacts and transactions with the firms with which it has common directors. Among the proxy statements of the 100 top industrials for 1957, I was able to find only one significant policy statement on intercorporate relations. Republic Steel, in a statement that innumerable other corporations could have made just as well, frankly declared, "In accordance with the policy of the Corporation Messrs. White, Patton, Foy, and Hancock, as well as other officers of the Corporation, serve as officers and directors of certain companies in which the Corporation has a substantial (but not controlling) stock interest, from which it purchases raw materials and/or to which it has advanced funds for construction or exploration programs." The directors and major officers of Republic Steel each sit on an average of six other boards. No corporation in a position of dependency on one of the top 200 corporations can refuse the giant a seat on its board, and thus a potent voice in the guidance of its affairs, without risking the loss of an important, if not decisive, segment of its sales.

THE DIRECTORS

Now let us undertake to discover if the corporate director is, in fact, the passive yet statesmanlike creature that is portrayed by modern theories. To accomplish this, we shall examine in some detail the nature of power and control in the 100 largest industrial corporations, as ranked by assets, in 1957. (Of these, 72 were also in the top 100 in 1937.) These 100 corporations accounted for 54 per cent of the assets of the 200 largest nonfinancial corporations in 1957—compared to only 37 per cent in 1937—or about one-quarter of all non-financial corporation assets and one-tenth of total national assets.[8] The form and extent of control within these 100 corporations is significant, both in measuring the concentration of wealth within the very small elite and in evaluating the dominant theories on the nature of corporate power in America.

In the largest industrial corporations, the directors are neither a passive group nor at odds with the basic policies and interests of management. The reason is simple: Most company directors are also members of management. The trend in this direction has been decisive. In 1937–39, 36 per cent of the directors of the top industrials were also key officers in their respective companies. By 1957, that figure was 50 per cent. This meant, taking into account interlocking directorates, that the majority of the 1,477 directors of the 100 top companies were active officers in some of those companies. In 47 of the top 100, officer-directors held absolute majorities.[9] So with most directors, it is obvious how they exert power: They are actively engaged in the management of the largest corporations.

A National Industrial Conference Board study of directors of 638 manufacturing corporations of varied sizes in 1959, found that 46 per cent were officers as well as directors of their companies. Another 17 per cent were "substantial stockholders" who were not officers, and 10 per cent represented interested financial institutions.[10]

There remains the problem of how power is exercised by directors who are not also officers.

Some directors, as we have seen in our discussion of interlocking directorates, exert influence because they represent other, and usually larger, corporations. Backed by their primary company, they are in a position to demand conformity to certain policies. Whether or not they exert this power is immaterial. The fact is that they can.

For a director of one firm, obtaining a connection as director in other firms—and preferably a large number of them—is motivated by the realization that this power in reserve may be useful to his primary firm or himself. General Motors, for example, was helped in monopolizing the bus-manufacturing industry by the fact that a number of bankers sat on transit-company boards of directors. Eager for GM accounts, these bankers intervened with transit managers on behalf of GM buses.[11]

In 1939, the top officers and directors of each of the 97 largest manufacturing corporations collectively owned an average of 7.0 per cent of the *total* number of shares in their own company. This is a conservative estimate based on far more abundant data than are available for the present period.

Now let us investigate the stock ownership of directors. From the annual proxy statements and documents filed with the Securities and Exchange Commission, we can arrive at a *minimum* percentage for the ownership of *voting* stock by the directors of the 100 largest industrial corporations. In 1957, the board of directors of these corporations owned or represented an average of 9.9 per cent of its shares. That figure would probably be increased by several percentage points if it were possible to include the stock ownership in several closely owned giants that do not issue proxy statements. In only 23 of these 100 companies are directors listed as owning more than 10 per cent of the voting stock; in 36, they are listed as owning less than 1 per cent. As in 1937, the vast majority of stock owned by directors is held by no more than 300 men.[12]

The matter of stock ownership by directors only begins with the figure of 10 per cent. We know that large holdings are synonymous with power; however, their absence does not necessarily rule out the presence of power in some subtler or more complex form. It is much more likely that we are ignorant of crucial information. It is important to press the matter further, to persevere in the search for the location of such power by assuming that it is not necessarily diffused.

Let us first look back a generation, and examine the 1937–39 directorates of the 72 of 1957's 100 top industrials for which we have information. It is quite clear that many of the important stockholding groups of the late 1930's are still in the same controlling positions. In board after board, the same family names appear in 1957 and in 1937–39—even when these people are no longer listed as having significant stock holdings. It is especially intriguing to find that the family pattern is very noticeable in 22 of the 72 corporations, and that in 1957, these 22 had an average stock ownership by directors of only 3.1 per cent, which very substantially pulled down the over-all average.

The splitting of blocks of stocks among family members for tax purposes, or the placing of the stocks in professionally managed trusts and investment companies, where identities can be obscured, may have practical value for the corporate elite. But these moves can hardly be regarded as significant changes in stock ownership.

In 1937–39 the Phipps family, via Bessemer Securities Corporation, owned 9.7 per cent of the stock of International Paper. In 1957, Ogden Phipps, chairman of Bessemer, sat on the International Paper board and was listed as owning 0.1 per cent of its stock. The Mellon family owned more than

50 per cent of Gulf Oil in 1937–39, but the two Mellons who sat on Gulf's board in 1957 were listed as owning a mere 6.5 per cent. The Mathers owned 9.3 per cent of Youngstown Sheet and Tube in 1937–39, but were listed, through their one director, as owning only 0.5 per cent in 1957.

The Du Ponts owned 15 per cent of U.S. Rubber in 1937–39, but in 1957, their representative, G. P. Edwards, who sat on the board was listed as owning virtually nothing. The Jones, Laughlin, and Robinson families owned about one-third of the Jones & Laughlin stock in 1937–39, but in 1957, their three board seats derived from their combined ownership of 0.5 per cent. The McCormick family owned about one-third of International Harvester in 1937–39, but the two family members on the board in 1957 owned a mere 1.2 per cent. The Levis family owned 16.8 per cent of Owens-Illinois Glass in 1937–39; they had two board members but less than 1.5 per cent of the stock in 1957. The Root family held 3.6 per cent of this company's stock in 1937–39, but in 1957, its one director was listed for about 0.3 per cent.

In search of some definition of the top elite, Robert A. Gordon, in *Business Leadership in the Large Corporation* (1945), took the 20 largest shareholders—including banks, trusts, foundations, insurance, and other corporations, as well as individuals—of each of the 200 largest corporations in 1937–39 (as determined by the TNEC), which he pruned to 176 by eliminating subsidiaries. He found that the cumulative top 20 stockholders owned an average of 28.6 per cent of the market value of common stock. In 101 out of 183 stock issues, they owned at least 20 per cent, or what is for all practical purposes a controlling share. Individuals or their legal devices, such as trusts and personal holding companies, owned half of the stock held by this tiny group of no more than 4,000 shareholders. In effect, they were the dominant shareowner influence in corporate affairs.[13]

Here the concentration of stock ownership in a small group

is plainly seen. But what it means in terms of economic power is less clear. It is debatable how much this group can do toward obtaining control, if they do not already have it, over the corporations they own. However, the large increase in the number of corporate proxy fights in recent years and the success of insurgents in about one-third of these indicate that the power of key stockholders is no myth.[14]

In many corporations whose stock is highly concentrated in a very small group, key stockholders choose not to exert power through direct representation on the board of directors and in top officer groups. Obviously their major concern as stockholders is profits and investment security, which, as indicated by the consistently high net corporate income and the restricted distribution of dividends to lower personal taxes, has been well served by the existing officers and directors. Since no major American corporation has ever sought to pursue a policy of enlightened public activities at the cost of basic profit margins, stockholders have never been forced to exert power for this reason.

The power of both stockholders and managers, however, exists within a small elite whose relation to society is rarely changed by disputes within its own ranks. In 1937–39, there was no visible center of control through ownership in only 58 of the top 176 corporations. In 83 corporations, ultimate power rested with family stockholding groups, some owning as little as 4 per cent and actively involved in management, most owning much more and inactive. Thirty-five companies were dominated by corporate groups who were in turn owned by large shareholders.[15]

Because of the continued, if not intensified, concentration of shares in a very small proportion of the stockholders, it must be concluded that the most powerful corporate giants still remain within the control of a small group of men. This was at least as true in 1957 as in the late 1930's, since the means of control have become more centralized in the intervening years.

MANAGEMENT

Berle and Means have alleged that the top officers of the giant corporations no longer own any significant percentage of the stock and that, as professional managers, they do not have the same interests as the stockholders. The new managers, it is claimed, are oriented toward rationalizing and consolidating the position of the corporation, are more sensitive to public opinion, and are concerned with avoiding risk ventures that might maximize profits but would endanger the basic security of the corporation.

Whether the "great faceless corporations [are] 'owned' by no one and run by self-designated 'managers' " can be settled by the answers to two crucial questions that have been ignored by the theorists: (1) How much stock do the key managers own in the top corporations they run? (2) How much stock does management, as a class, own in all corporations, and thus to what extent do they share the profit motive of stockholders? Is it true, as corporation lawyer David T. Bazelon put it, that the manager of the giant corporation is "not a capitalist at all; he is a new fish?"[16]

The issue here is not the concentration of economic power but the motivation of managerial actions by tangible incentives. However small their percentage of the stock may be, it is exceedingly important to their personal fortunes and, therefore, a crucial motivating factor in their corporate role. In early 1957, 25 General Motors officers owned an average of 11,500 shares each.[17] Collectively, their holdings would have been inconsequential if they had chosen to try to obtain control of GM through their stocks. Yet each of these men had a personal stake of roughly a half million dollars in the company—plus the tantalizing prospect that over the next decade or two the corporation's growth and profits might double or treble the value of his stock and make him an exceptionally wealthy man.

The corporate executive is tied to the profit performance of the corporate system in many tangible ways. But the discussions by Berle, Riesman, and others of the separation of management from the profit incentive, and from stock in particular, is based on a failure to appreciate the nature of the executive compensation system. Most serious of all, they have ignored the major, and potentially revolutionary, impact of the stock option on the corporate executive.

The stock option, originated in 1950, has committed top management more strongly than ever before to the corporation's profit position, because without profits, the options are largely worthless. By 1957, option plans had been instituted by 77 per cent of the manufacturing corporations listed on the New York or American Stock Exchanges. Of the 100 largest industrials, only 13 did not have option plans in 1959, and in most of these corporations, there was heavy stock ownership by directors. Of the 87 with option plans, the 83 for which public data was available had granted key officers options on an average of 1.9 per cent of their outstanding voting stock by 1959.[18]

Suggestive of future trends is the percentage of outstanding stock reserved for executive options. By 1960, Inland Steel had assigned the equivalent of 11 per cent of its outstanding voting stock for options. Ford, in 1960, reserved 6.7 per cent of its outstanding shares for future options. If this trend continues, it will further strengthen the tie between management and stock, especially in companies whose management holdings are now comparatively small.

Top corporation executives are very well-paid men. In 1958, the median income for the highest-paid 1,700 was $73,600.[19] But Berle and the others assume that they, unlike most others in this income class, will not buy stock. The fact is that the corporate executive *does* buy stock. Thus his personal fortunes are bound not only to the money-making success of his own company but also to that of the larger corporate structure in which he has invested. Theoretically, it would not make a great deal of difference if the managers had, in fact, no personal interest in the dividend performance or market value of stocks, since it has never been shown how the managers differ, in practice and theory, from the stockholding elite.

In fact, the managerial class is the largest single group in the stockholding population, and a greater proportion of this class owns stock than any other. The statistics: 44.8 per cent of all administrative officials—top company officials and managers in corporations, banks, and the like—own stock. For operating supervisory officials—managers of medium-size and small companies, department heads of these companies or larger organizations, and kindred types—the figure was 19.4 per cent. These are the results of the Brookings Institution's 1952 census of stockholders, which also showed that 6.3 per cent of all shareholders were administrative executives and 13.1 per cent were operating supervisory officials.[20]

How much stock does the managerial class own? We know that spending units owning $100,000 or more in marketable stock in 1949 accounted for at least 65 to 71 per cent of the total individual ownership, and we can reasonably assume that this figure is valid after 1949, since stock concentration has been fairly stable. Of all the spending units in that category in 1957, nearly half—47.4 per cent, to be precise—were from the managerial class. Also, one-fifth of the managerial spending units owning stock in 1957 possessed more than $100,000 worth.[21]

It is impossible to give a precise figure on the percentage of stock owned by the managerial class, but these figures indicate that the managers own a very large proportion, if not well over the majority, of shares in the United States.

Management, then, is the class most interested in the highest dividends, in both their own firms and others. And taking into account the greater prevalence of stock ownership among top management shown by the Brookings study, as well as the high incomes and stock options in this group, it becomes clear that the interest of top executives in stock is undoubtedly the most important among those in the managerial class.

To talk of a separation between management and major stockholders in the United States is obviously quite impossible; they are virtually one and the same.

The concentration of economic power in a very small elite is an indisputable fact. This power is a function of both their direct ownership in the corporate structure and their ability to control it. Their possession of savings and wealth is possible because of the continuing basic inequality of income that is simply a part of a larger pattern of inequality in the United States.

The implications of this intense centralization of economic power are twofold. First, the concentration of income allocates a large share of the consumption of goods to a small proportion of the population. For a public policy directed toward maintenance of full employment through full consumption, this fact raises major obstacles for working within the existing income distribution structure. Second, and more important for this study, a social theory assuming a democratized economic system—or even a trend in this direction—is quite obviously not in accord with social reality. Whether the men who control industry are socially responsive or trustees of the social welfare is quite another matter; it is one thing to speculate about their motivations, another to generalize about economic facts. And even if we assume that these men act benevolently toward their workers and the larger community, their actions still would not be the result of social control through a formal democratic structure and group participation, which are the essentials for democracy; they would be an arbitrary *noblesse oblige* by the economic elite. When discussing the existing corporate system, it would be more realistic to drop all references to democracy.

The real questions are: (1) Do a small group of very wealthy men have the power to guide industry, and thereby much of the total economy, toward ends that they decide upon as compatible with their own interests? (2) Do they own and control the major corporations?

The answers must inevitably be affirmative.

5

The Causes of Poverty

The West Virginia worker left behind in a virtually deserted mining town, without sufficient money to buy the minimum food needed to supplement his "mollygrub" (his name for Federal surplus food), lives in a state of poverty. The slum dweller in the Scoville area of Cleveland or the South End of Boston, unable to afford housing with adequate heating and sanitation, also lives in poverty. The laid-off Detroit auto worker, forced to turn to charity handouts for clothes for his family after exhausting his unemployment checks and savings, is another of the poor. There are the chronically poor, including most Southern dirt-farmers, families headed by women, and textile workers, and there are the circulating poor, including laid-off auto workers, some of the ill, and the family with a moderate income but too many children consuming it. Poverty is the economic inability to maintain minimum standards of medical care, nourishment, housing, and clothing.

Despite inequitable distribution of all forms of wealth in America, the reader may reasonably ask whether poverty has nonetheless been eliminated. And he may go on to inquire to what extent this inequality is a reflection of sociological factors such as age, occupation, and race, rather than of purely economic ones. The answers to these questions will be relevant in determining whether broad income inequality can exist without causing large-scale human and social problems and in judging the present economy's distributive effectiveness and its value in human and utilitarian terms.

There is a general, although undocumented, impression that poverty in the United States is not very extensive or serious. It is the common opinion of social scientists that, as Max Lerner wrote in *America as a Civilization* (1957): "The poverty in America, in fact, is almost entirely outside the economic sphere proper."[1] Poverty is of two major types, according to John Kenneth Galbraith: "insular poverty," in a community or region made up of people who are reluctant to move; and "case poverty," made up of mental deficients, alcoholics, and the like—people who are not motivated to "get ahead" because of "qualities of personality," as Talcott Parsons put it.[2] "Millions of families in our industrial cities and towns, and on the farms," Frederick Lewis Allen claimed, "have been lifted from poverty or near-poverty to a status where they can enjoy what has been traditionally considered a middle-class way of life. . . ."[3] David Riesman referred to this "middle class" as the "overprivileged two-thirds."

According to such social theory, a sharp decline in the extent of poverty in the United States was the happy result of some radical alterations in the economy—particularly the greater income equality.

Sociologist Seymour Lipset asserted: "The assembly line and mass production, with the higher wages and more equal distribution of wealth that they make possible, are thus probably more responsible for the development of the American 'classless' society than trends in social mobility."[4] Sociologists Nelson N. Foote and Paul K. Hatt concluded that "net occupational movement has been toward the jobs of higher prestige," and accompanying this prestige is greater income. "Incomes tend to stabilize and equalize as salaries predominate," they claimed, and the number of salaried workers has been increasing.[5] Among blue-collar workers, they observed, the income differentials between skilled and unskilled workers have "narrowed appreciably."

But do these and similar assertions, as optimistic as they may be, have any basis in fact? To answer this question, we shall first re-evaluate the traditional causes of poverty—low wages, unemployment, etc. But seemingly non-economic factors, especially age, also have a significant effect on income, so we must evaluate them, too. Then, having analyzed the extent of poverty resulting from all causes, we shall consider other possible mitigating factors, such as a growing consumer credit, that are operating to reduce the extent of poverty in America today. Only when this is done will the human cost of the present inequitable distribution of economic resources become fully apparent.

WAGES AND UNEMPLOYMENT

It requires only a bag of corn meal, thirty pounds of flour, two pounds of rice, and ten pounds of butter to supply one-third of the monthly minimum dietary requirements for a family of four, according to a West Virginia Health Department estimate. But in 1959, more than 300,000 persons in that state depended on Federal handouts of these staples for their continued existence. For more than a decade, similar idle mining areas in Kentucky have had the same problems and the same futile hope of permanent improvements. And throughout the country about 2 million farm wage-workers earn roughly $750 a year on which to support their families; a third of these are migrants, who are invariably forced onto some type of relief each year.

In the spring of 1958, when *The Affluent Society* was published, some 5.5 million unemployed workers would probably have been skeptical about the optimism of its author, economist John Kenneth Galbraith. In late 1958, industrial output was 35 per cent greater than in 1948, but employment of production workers was 6 per cent lower. Specific industries were hard hit. Textile output in 1959 was 15 per cent greater than in 1948, employment 30 per cent lower. In the auto industry, output rose 65 per cent from 1947 to 1960 but the employment of production workers dropped 6 per cent, and although the output of raw steel increased 3 per cent from 1950 to 1960, employment of production workers fell 14 per cent. New England, in its textile cities, was on its way to becoming the West Virginia of the 1960's—and there was still no solution in sight for West Virginia. Detroit also presented a grim picture in early 1959. Although automobile production was well ahead of that of 1958, heavy unemployment existed, relief rolls were climbing, and more than 200,000 were aiding their diet with Federal "mollygrub." In Detroit, Pittsburgh, Buffalo, Akron, Flint, and numerous other cities, the seeds of future West Virginias were being sown. Even as production climbed, automation and technological advances stimulated intense problems and a disturbingly persistent high level of national unemployment. Shorter recovery periods between recessions have been the result.

Despite increased unionization and the uneven "full employment" that has followed World War II, large segments of the American workers still receive poverty wages. Of course, the line of demarcation between a poverty wage and a low annual wage is arbitrary, but for illustrative purposes, I will abandon the commonly accepted $2,000 a year—a criterion unchanged despite the postwar inflation—and take the more realistic $3,000. Among men employed in March, 1958, in *all* occupations and in *every* industry, 30 per cent earned less than $3,000 in 1957. Among those unemployed in March, 1958, however, nearly twice that percentage had earned less than $3,000 in 1957. And although this 30 per cent ignores the distinctions among industries, shown in Table VI (page 74), and among occupations, it is quite clear that a consider-

TABLE VI

PERCENTAGE OF MEN IN EACH MAJOR INDUSTRY GROUP
EARNING LESS THAN $3,000 IN 1957*

(100 = Total Employed per Group)

Public administration	9
Mining	14
Manufacturing	17
Transportation, communications, and other public utilities	18
Wholesale trade	20
Finance, insurance, and real estate	24
Professional and related services	29
Construction	30
Business and repair services	31
Retail trade	39
Entertainment and recreation services	46
Personal services	58
Agriculture, forestry, and fisheries	75
Total employed for all industries	30
Total unemployed for all industries	56

* Data refer to workers employed in March, 1958.

Source: Bureau of the Census, *Current Population Reports,* Series P-60, No. 30, pp. 38–39.

able proportion of the male work force has a meager income. Among employed women, the percentage earning less than $3,000 was very substantially higher.

It is important to note the limitations of Federal minimum-wage legislation. For one thing, it has never been applied to those industries most in need of even its conservative standards. In September, 1953, only 3 per cent of the retail-trade workers, for example, were covered, even though many worked for such giant corporations as the Great Atlantic & Pacific Tea Company, Sears, Roebuck, and J. C. Penney.[6] After the minimum wage had increased to $1 an hour, 26 per cent of the excluded retail-trade workers earned less than the minimum.[7] The new minimum wage law of

1961 brought 2 million retail workers under its coverage, but still left two-thirds totally unprotected. As in the past, this was again a story of too little, too late.

Conversely, those who are covered by the law usually do not need it. When the Federal minimum wage was raised to $1 an hour in 1956, only 2 million out of the 24 million covered (out of an employed nonagricultural labor force of 52 million) were earning less than $1 per hour.

Characteristically, the minimum wage is set well below prevailing wages and well below wages sufficient to provide a decent standard of living for the average family. In seven low-wage competitive industries surveyed by the U.S. Bureau of Labor Statistics, the $1 minimum did cause a large spurt in the number earning from $1 to $1.05 an hour. But despite this not-inconsequential improvement for the lowest-paid, they still received extremely low incomes. The proportion earning less than $1.25 an hour was 48 per cent before the law, 42 per cent after it.[8] The wage increases of workers already above the $1.25 level were moderate and normal.

The passage of the new minimum wage law in May, 1961, was a belated and essentially inconsequential effort to correct a few of the more glaring deficiencies in the existing minimum-wage laws. Although 3.6 million new workers were brought under the law, this increase meant that about 50 per cent of the nonagricultural wage and salary workers were covered, compared to 46 per cent in 1956. Of the newly covered workers, only 663,000 were earning less than $1 an hour, and this will be their minimum hourly wage until September, 1964, when it will be increased to $1.15, and then to $1.25 in September, 1965. But in early 1961, $1 was worth only 91 cents in 1956 purchasing power, and $1.25 was worth only $1.14. By 1965, at the present rate of inflation, $1.25 will be worth about $1 in 1956 purchasing power. For nearly 2 million workers already covered by the law, wages will be increased to $1.15 until September, 1963, when they will be raised to $1.25. In reality, recent advances in minimum-wage legislation, whether for previously or newly covered workers, have scarcely kept up with inflation.

Furthermore, instead of making progressive gains for the worker, the minimum wage has failed to keep pace with present levels. Just to equal the 1939 relationship of minimum wage to actual average wage of manufacturing workers would have required a minimum wage of $1.37 in 1959. And since 1939, the relationship of the minimum wage to the actual average hourly wage paid to the vast bulk of workers has made it even less significant in procuring a decent living standard for all. In 1939, the minimum wage was two-thirds of the average manufacturing worker's hourly pay, but in 1961, the new, increased minimum wage was no more than one-half the average manufacturing worker's hourly wage.

It is worth noting at this point that in 1956, 34 per cent of the under-$3,000 income class was composed of farmers and farm labor; 47 per cent of farm-operating families earned less than $2,000, and 65 per cent earned less than $3,000.[9] These facts clash sharply with the popular notion. "All but the unluckiest and least provident of the farmers were living decently," wrote historian Eric Goldman, "often amid so many machines that a nine-to-five work day, with a television evening, was possible for both husband and wife."[10] But the statistics contradict the commonly accepted picture of the average contemporary farmer as prosperously driving about in an expensive automobile bought with parity payments. In reality, a mere 2 per cent of the farms accounted for 42 per cent of the total acreage in 1950. Further, only 9 per cent of the farmers received 50 per cent of the price-support money in 1953. By 1958, the net income of the average farm family, adjusted for inflation, was only 15 per cent higher than the 1937–41 average.[11] Over the course of twenty years, the average farmer has barely held his ground against inflation.

The real income—the actual purchasing power—of workers in major industries has generally increased since 1939, although this has not eliminated low incomes. This rising trend is somewhat exaggerated because annual incomes for 1939 were abnormally low, and because the available data is based on weekly real incomes (of the employed), which overstate annual real income by not fully taking unemployment into account. Nonetheless, these statistics show that most of the increase was due to the rapid rise in weekly hours and employment during wartime 1939–44, and that growth in real income since 1944 has been minor. The gross, after-tax, average weekly real income of production workers employed in manufacturing, who accounted for one-quarter of the nonagricultural wage and salary workers, increased 53 per cent from 1939 through 1944, but only 17 per cent from 1944 through 1960. Rising real income since 1939 must be attributed primarily to the war, and not to the postwar period.[12]

The average increase in gross weekly real income from 1939 through 1957 for production and nonsupervisory workers was 129 per cent in bituminous-coal mining (where the number employed greatly declined), 74 per cent in building construction, 46 per cent in Class I railroads, 17 per cent in telephone companies, 40 per cent in wholesale trade, 34 per cent in retail trade, and 22 per cent in laundries. Increases in hourly real income were generally somewhat lower, because the weekly increase in income was partly the result of a rise in the number of hours worked per year. From 1914 to 1929, the average manufacturing worker's *annual* real income increased 40 per cent. This is an average annual increase of 2.7 per cent, as compared to an average annual increase of 3.6 per cent in 1939–60, the latter being calculated on a significantly more generous weekly basis. Since 1944, the average annual increase in real income has been much smaller.[13]

National real-income averages present the same pattern: a

rapid increase from 1939 to 1944, and a relatively slow rise thereafter. Discussing average family real income from 1929 to 1955, the Bureau of Labor Statistics wrote: "Compared with 1929, average [family] real income measured in constant dollars has increased roughly 30 per cent; 40 per cent on a per capita basis, reflecting the smaller size of the family."[14]

It is probable that the lower-income brackets, which gained most from the full employment accompanying World War II, have received the bulk of increases in family real income that occurred from 1939 through 1944, and that the major increases during the postwar period went to the middle- and higher-income classes. The percentage of families and unattached individuals earning $2,000 or less (in 1948 dollars) declined only from 33 to 31 per cent from 1948 through 1954, while those earning $5,000-plus increased from 17 to 25 per cent.[15] This uneven distribution of real-income gains only serves to increase income inequality and poverty.

Periodic unemployment, a built-in feature of our business-cycle economy, is a guarantee of low income and poverty. It strikes the same major group each time; the majority of the periodically unemployed are invariably unskilled and semi-skilled workers, who are traditionally subject to layoffs and seasonal unemployment. The unemployment rate among unskilled workers was 34 per cent in 1940, 12 per cent in 1950, but 20 per cent during the recession in early 1961. Among semiskilled workers, it was 13 per cent in 1940, 6 per cent in 1950, and 12 per cent in early 1961. Skilled workers fared better, with an unemployment rate of 15 per cent in 1940, 6 per cent in 1950, and 10 per cent in early 1961. In contrast, the unemployment rate among clerical and sales workers in early 1961 was a mere 5 per cent.[16]

The significant fact is that since World War II, a very substantial number of all blue-collar workers have worked less than 50 weeks a year. Take 1949, for example: only 66 per cent of the skilled, 60 per cent of the semiskilled, and 50 per cent of the unskilled were employed 50 weeks or more —a fact one must remember when the high hourly wage of, say, hod carriers is cited.[17]

Among men who were unemployed in March, 1958, 38 per cent had earned less than $2,000 in 1957, and 56 per cent had earned less than $3,000. Those who were laid off more than two weeks in 1957 had received less than two-thirds the income for the year of the fully employed men.[18]

Contrary to popular belief, unemployment compensation has had no fundamental effect on poverty caused by periodic unemployment. Its ability to prevent families of jobless workers from slipping further down the income scale is open to question. For one thing, it covers only 60 per cent of the labor force, leaving a solid 40 per cent unprotected. Inflation has had an undermining effect. Although a week's unemployment compensation was originally intended to equal half the average week's pay (each state decides its own amount), it amounted to only one-third of the weekly pay during the 1950's. In 1960, the national average weekly compensation was $32.75, too little to maintain even a single person at a decent standard of living. Forty per cent of the 8.5 million different family heads who were unemployed at some time between June, 1957, and June, 1958, did not collect compensation; half of those who did exhausted their benefits before re-employment.[19]

To the worker without a job, the first need—if he is one of the fortunate 60 per cent covered by unemployment compensation—is to supplement these limited payments by dipping into whatever ready savings he has. If his jobless state continues, he may have to borrow money and cash in his insurance. Meanwhile, his standard of living declines as he tries to cut expenses. At some point, he exhausts his unemployment compensation. Ultimately, he may be forced to seek relief in some form. One study of unemployed workers in 1954 showed that 12 per cent of the single earners and 27 per cent of those who were the head of a four-person family eventually went on relief.[20]

The entire unemployment-compensation system is based on the assumption that there will never be a prolonged recession, much less a serious depression. It is interesting to speculate what might happen to it in the event of a serious recession of substantial duration. The system is completely financed by a payroll tax of up to 2.7 per cent on the first $3,000 earned in a year by each worker, and is paid by every employer with eight or more workers. When a company's rate of discharge increases, the payroll tax can be increased by the state, to the maximum of 2.7 per cent; however, the size of the payroll has probably decreased meanwhile, and there will be less to tax. Since at least two-thirds of all such payroll costs are passed on to the public in higher prices, low- and middle-income earners eventually finance most of the system.

Each state has its own reserve fund, and the total of all these reserve funds is usually less than a tenth of the nation's annual taxable wages. These funds are completely independent of each other, and reserves built up in one state cannot be distributed to the unemployed in another state. In a number of postwar years, the funds' outlays have been greater than their income. Certainly, a national total reserve of less than $7 billion, which was true of 1959, would do little to sustain worker purchasing power during substantial unemployment in an economy with normal wages and salaries of $257 billion, which was the figure for 1958. Pennsylvania, plagued by minor unemployment from 1949 through 1958, collected more than it paid out in only two of ten years. Finally in 1958, when one-tenth of its labor force was jobless at some time during the year, Pennsylvania's unemployment reserve fund was nearly bankrupted. Only a Federal loan, part of an emergency program, saved it.

This 1958 temporary program of Federal loans, undertaken to enable states to lengthen the compensation period from the then-current average of 26 weeks to 39 weeks, was largely a failure because of the unwillingness of most states to acquire new debts. Only 17 states participated. The Federal loans did not change the basic weaknesses in the financial structure of the compensation system—except possibly to add to them by burdening the funds with indebtedness—and the temporary 1961 plan is essentially identical to the 1958 measure.

Company supplementary unemployment-compensation plans, although an important aid to the limited number of workers they cover, suffer from all the shortcomings of the government plan, plus the limited liability protection assumed by companies in all such arrangements.

In his important study *Personal Income During Business Cycles* (1956), Daniel Creamer concludes: "During the 1948–1949 business contraction, compensation to the unemployed offset about one-fifth of the loss in total payrolls and about one-eighth of the loss in disposable income, defined to exclude compensation to the unemployed."[21] Similarly, in the early 1958 recession, unemployment compensation offset only about one-fifth of the lost paychecks.

Such fractional success hardly deserves the confidence expressed by many sociologists in the ability of unemployment compensation to protect the unemployed, and society, from the inevitable fluctuations of the business cycle.

OCCUPATIONAL AND ECONOMIC CLASS

Recent theories on the class structure in America have taken for granted, and rightly so, the close interrelationship of income, occupation, and prestige. Some sociologists have suggested that the presumably expanding middle-class income has also meant a growing middle-class prestige. But before the concept of America as a middle-class nation can be proved, a number of important questions must be answered: Has the economic position of the working class improved recently in relation to the middle class? What occupations now make up the low-income classes? How mobile is a spending unit's position in the lowest- or highest-income class, and to what degree is its position a reflection of such changing factors as age and sex?

Anyone seeking to locate the American middle class will have a difficult time, primarily because the income inequalities separating the three major blue-collar classes have not narrowed over the past three decades and the three groups have not moved any closer to a vague and amorphous middle class. Meanwhile, white-collar workers have moved toward relatively lower income levels. Save for this, the traditional income standings by occupation have not changed substantially. Although by no means all blue-collar workers earned no more than $3,000 in 1956, 46 per cent of the family heads in that income group were semiskilled and unskilled workers, or service workers (such as domestics, barbers, and firemen).

A sharp inequality exists in the incomes of the major occupational groupings, a difference that is marked not only when the earnings of the unskilled, service, and farm workers are contrasted to those of the managerial and professional classes, but also when these low incomes are compared to the incomes of skilled workers (see Table VII).

Within the blue-collar class, the income gaps between the unskilled, semiskilled, and skilled workers have remained fairly constant, but with the decreased unemployment since 1939, all three groups have significantly improved their positions vis-à-vis clerical and sales workers.

If the income-tenth rankings of specific blue-collar occupations, such as carpentry and welding, are calculated, a clear relationship between income-tenth and occupation can be

TABLE VII

RELATIVE AVERAGE 1958 INCOME OF HEADS OF SPENDING
UNITS, BY OCCUPATIONAL CLASSES

(100 = Income of Clerical and Sales Workers)

Farm operators	56
Unskilled and service workers	57
Semiskilled workers	90
Clerical and sales workers	100
Skilled workers	120
Self-employed businessmen	127
Professional and semiprofessional workers	149
Managerial workers	153

Source: Federal Reserve Bulletin, July, 1959, p. 714. About one-tenth of all spending units were headed by women. Most of them belonged to the clerical-and-sales or semiskilled group, which tended to depress the earnings of these groups.

seen. Most skilled occupations are in the fourth or fifth income-tenth—a long way from the top but just within the wealthier half of the nation. Most of the semiskilled are in the fifth or sixth income-tenth, or roughly in the middle. Most of the service or unskilled workers are in the sixth, seventh, or eighth income-tenth, or close to the bottom of the income scale. These findings are based on occupational averages and ignore substantial inequalities within specific occupations that could place the highest and lowest earners in different income-tenths. These inequalities are generally greatest in those blue-collar occupations in which acquired seniority and skills—in a word, age—are most crucial to earning power.*

When the occupations for which we have historical earnings data are ranked in income-tenths over the years, the remarkable stability of their positions since 1935 becomes strikingly evident. Key professionals have remained in the

* All data are from Appendix 1, pp. 135–39.

highest income-tenths. Blue-collar workers, despite the impact of unionization, have experienced at best minor changes in their position. Unionization has not been able to change significantly the income-tenth ranking of the workers in the industries covered. In large part, this is true because the market standing of an industry, and its consequent ability to absorb and grant wage increases, is only rarely affected by unionization.[22] (See Table VIII.)

Income mobility, which every worker experiences in a fairly predictable pattern, is most commonly a function of age, and will be discussed in that context later in this chapter. Less frequently, it reflects an inflationary increase that does nothing more than raise a worker's income from, say, $2,900 to $3,050, thus boosting him into the next income class. Occasionally, it results from an unusual occurrence, like an inheritance, a sale of capital assets, or the loss of a lawsuit.

George Katona and Janet A. Fisher, in a study of a group of families and unattached individuals over a period of two years (1947 and 1948), show that in the $0–$1,000 and $1,000–$2,000 income classes, about two-thirds of the spending units remained in the same class. Of the one-third that were mobile, almost all shifted into an adjoining class. In fact, at the end of the two years, more than 90 per cent of the families in every income class could be found in their original or an adjoining income class: 51 per cent were in the same income class, 27 per cent were in the next-higher income class, and 13 per cent were in the next-lower income class; only 4 per cent had climbed two or more income classes higher, and 5 per cent had dropped two or more income classes.[24] Considering that in 1948 prices were 8 per cent higher than in 1947, and extensive wage adjustments occurred, the change was minimal.

Similarly, Simon Kuznets, in his study of the top 5 per cent in income, suggests that the individual income-shares within this top group—with no change in individual members during his study—vary only slightly over a two- or three-

TABLE VIII

OCCUPATIONS RANKED BY INCOME-TENTH,* 1929–52 [23]

(Based on Average Annual Income)

Occupational Groups	1929	1935–36	1949	1951	1952
Lawyers	1	1	1	1	
Physicians	1	1	1	1	
Dentists	2+	1	1	1	
Full professors (large state university)	2+	1			2+
Associate professors (large state university)	2—	2+			2—
High-school principals†	1	1	1	1	
High-school teachers†	3+	1	2—	3+	
Elementary-school teachers†	4	2—	3	4	
Social workers	5	3	5—		
Ministers	4	3—	6		
Nurses	6—	6—	6		
Engineers	1	1	2		
Skilled and semiskilled workers (by industry)‡					
Automobile	6	5+	5		
Chemical	7+	5—	5		
Machine and machine tools	6—	5	5		
Furniture	7	6+	7—		
Iron and steel	5—	6+	5—		
Paper and pulp	6	6+	5—		
Unskilled workers (by industry)					
Automobile	7	6+	6+		
Chemical	7	7+	6		
Machine and machine tools	8	7	6—		
Furniture	8—	8	8		
Iron and steel	7	8	6—		
Paper and pulp	8	8+	6—		

* Income-tenths are ranked in descending order: 1 equals the highest tenth, 10 the lowest tenth, etc. A plus or minus sign indicates the highest or lowest third within the income-tenth.

† Cities of more than 500,000.

‡ Average of combined incomes.

year period, and that those dropping out of the top 5 per cent still remain close to the top.[25]

The declining economic position of clerical and sales workers has been a major factor in increasing the extent of poverty since World War II. This slump has been largely due to the lag in real income among workers in the whole-sale and retail trades and the failure of clerical and sales workers to keep up with inflation through collective bargaining. However, they are much less subject to loss of pay from unemployment than are blue-collar workers.

The importance of this downward trend in the relative income of clerical and sales workers is deepened by their growing share in the labor force. They comprised 10.5 per cent of the labor force in 1910, 16.5 per cent in 1940, and 19.7 per cent in 1955.[26] Since 1940, the number of clerical and sales workers has risen more than twice as fast as the number of blue-collar workers, a trend that will surely be spurred by the increasing automation of technology, expansion of government functions, and mounting number of women who head families. Thus, the declining relative economic position of clerical and sales workers can be expected to be of increasing import; it will very probably broaden the extent of low incomes and poverty in the future.

AGE AND INCOME

The relationship between age and income is only casually appreciated by recent theories on the purported redistribution of income. It is known, of course, that the average person's income begins to decline after he is fifty-five years of age, and that it declines sharply after sixty-five. In 1957, 58 per cent of the spending units headed by persons sixty-five years and older earned less than $2,000. The relationship between old age and low income has often been considered a reflection of sociological rather than economic factors—and therefore not to be included in any study of the economy. Actually, the character of the relationship is too integrated to be dissected. However, its significance is mounting with the increase in the number of older persons. The lowest-income groups include a heavy concentration of older persons—in 1957, one-third of all spending units in the $0–$2,000 class were headed by persons sixty-five years and older; in 1948, it was 28 per cent.[27]

But in economic planning and social policy, it must be remembered that, with the same income, the sixty-five-or-more spending unit will not spend less or need less than the younger spending unit, even though the pressure to save is greater than on the young.[28] The functional ethos of our economy dictates that the comparatively unproductive old-age population should consume in accordance with their output rather than their requirements. Most social scientists have accepted these values; they have assumed that the minimum economic needs of the aged should be lower than those of the younger family. But it is precisely at retirement that personal requirements and the new demands of leisure call for an even larger income if this period is to be something more enjoyable than a wait for death.

The relationship between age and income is seen most clearly in the unionized blue-collar worker. Except for lay-offs, which his seniority minimizes, and wage increments for higher productivity, awarded in many industries, his income range is determined by his occupation. But within that income range, the deciding factor is the man's age. After forty-five, the average worker who loses his job has more difficulty in finding a new one. Despite his seniority, the older worker is likely to be downgraded to a lower-paying job when he can no longer maintain the pace set by younger men. This is especially true of unskilled and semiskilled workers.

The early and lower income period of a person's working life, during which he acquires his basic vocational skills, is most pronounced for the skilled, managerial, or professional worker. Then, between the ages of twenty-five and fifty, the average worker receives his peak earnings. Meanwhile, his family expenses rise; there are children to support and basic household durables to obtain. Although his family's income may rise substantially until he is somewhere between thirty-five and forty-five, per-capita consumption (see a 1950 study given in Appendix 2, pages 140–41) may drop at the same time. For the growing, working-class family, limited in income by the very nature of the breadwinner's occupation, the economic consequences of this parallel rise in age, income, and obligations are especially pressing. Many in the low-income classes are just as vulnerable to poverty during middle age, when they have a substantially larger income, as in old age. As family obligations finally do begin declining, so does income. Consequently, most members of these classes never have an adequate income.[29]

Thus we see that, for a time, increasing age means increasing income, and therefore a probable boost in income-tenth position. Although there are no extensive data on the matter, it can be confidently asserted that the higher income-tenths have a much greater representation of spending units headed by persons aged thirty-five to fifty-five than do the lower income-tenths. This is demonstrably the case among the richest 5 per cent of the consumer units.[30] The real question is, To what extent does distribution of income-tenths within a certain age group deviate from distribution of income-tenths generally? Although information is not as complete as might be desired, there is more than enough to make contingent generalizations. Detailed data exist on income distribution by tenths and by age for 1935–36 and 1948, and on income-size distribution by age for the postwar years.[31] They disclose sharp income inequalities within every age group (although more moderate in the eighteen-to-twenty-five category)—inequalities that closely parallel the over-all national income pattern. The implication is clear: A spending unit's income-tenth position *within his age category* varies much less, if at all, and is determined primarily by his occupation.

In other words, in America, the legendary land of eco-

nomic opportunity where any man can work his way to the
top, there is only slight income mobility outside the natural
age cycle of rising, then falling income. Since most of the
sixty-five-and-over age group falls into the low-income brackets
and constitutes the largest segment of the $0–$2,000 income
class, it is of obvious importance in analyzing future poverty
in the United States to examine the growth trends of this
group. The sixty-five-and-over population composed 4.0 per
cent of the total population in 1900, 5.3 per cent in 1930,
8.4 per cent in 1955, and will reach an estimated 9.6 per
cent in 1970 and 10.8 per cent in 2000. Between 1900 and
1975, the total national population is expected to increase
176 per cent, but those from ages forty-five through sixty-four
are expected to increase 315 per cent, and those sixty-five and
over are expected to increase 572 per cent. Between 1960
and 1975, the population aged eighteen to twenty-five is also
expected to grow far more rapidly than the middle-aged
population.[32] With the more rapid expansion of these two
low-income groups, the young and the old, in the years
immediately ahead, an increase in the extent of poverty is
probable.

It is revealing to look at the sources that provide the
meager income of the sixty-five-and-over population in the
United States. In 1958, the largest source was their own earnings, which accounted for 35 per cent of their total income.
More than one-third of the aged men and nearly one-tenth
of the aged women remained in the labor force throughout
the 1950's; most of the men not employed were too ill or too
weak to work.[33] Only 22 per cent of the total income of the
aged came from social insurance, and this went to fewer than
half of them. Another 7 per cent came from public assistance
—and this, plus social insurance, represented the total con-
tribution of the "welfare state." Only 14 per cent of the
income of the aged came from government-employee, veteran,
private, or union pension plans, but these pensions should

be growing in importance. The remainder of support for the aged was supplied by income-in-kind, savings, and food and shelter provided by children or other relatives.[34]

The economic condition of the aged and the secondary role of social insurance in supporting them indicate that the highly touted "welfare state" measures are both inadequate and misunderstood. The average old-age-insurance payment for the month of November, 1960, was a mere $74.02, too little to maintain even a semblance of economic decency. (And more than one-quarter of the labor force was not covered under the system.) Since 27 per cent of the spending units headed by persons sixty-five and over had no liquid assets whatsoever in early 1958, and another 27 per cent had only $1–$999, most of the aged were forced to choose among employment, dependence on children, and relief.[35]

Thus, for most persons, old age means economic desperation.

The Social Security Old-Age and Survivors Insurance was designed to enforce the Victorian virtue of thrift in American society. "Congress has made clear its intent that the old-age and survivors insurance program be self-supporting and actuarially sound," writes the Social Security Administration.[36] In the twenty-three-year period up to November, 1960, the system collected and accumulated in interest $83 billion and paid out in benefits and expenses only $62 billion.[37] And to guarantee that the program remain self-supporting in the future, the OASI tax on income, according to present plans, will gradually increase from its present flat rate of 2.5 per cent to 4.5 per cent in 1969. Furthermore, the schedule of payments is arranged so that top income-earners will receive maximum benefits even though the OASI taxes none of their income after $4,800. For a man or woman earning $400 a month after 1950, for example, the monthly retirement benefit after sixty-five will be $127. The person who averaged $200 a month will receive $84, even though the OASI tax, being regressive like all flat-rate taxes, took a larger income percentage from him than from the middle- or high-income earner, who will receive the maximum benefit. Thus the system perpetuates after retirement much of the inequality of incomes that existed before.

THE CHANGING ROLE OF WOMEN

A major, but overlooked, element contributing to the growth of low-income classes and poverty in the past decade has been the increase in the number of families headed by women. From 1950 to 1957, the number of American families increased by 11.3 per cent, but the number headed by women was nearly double that. In 1935–36, 3.6 per cent of all households were headed by women; in 1956, it was 8.5 per cent, and this percentage can be expected to rise significantly in the next decade. This sociological trend has had economic consequences that have not been fully appreciated by students of poverty and income distribution.

The major cause of this trend, of course, is the break-up of marriages. There was 1 divorce for every 4 marriages in the mid-1950's. In 1940, 1.6 per cent of women had been divorced; in 1956, the percentage was half again as high, or 2.4 per cent. In recent years, almost as many couples have resorted to the "poor man's divorce"—separation—as have been legally divorced. Another factor has been the sharp upsurge in illegitimate births—from 88,000 recorded in 1938 to 205,000 in 1958.[38]

This trend toward households headed by women can only increase poverty. As is well known, employed women in general get less pay than men. More than one-third of working women are clerical and sales workers. Another third are semiskilled workers, mainly in factories, or service workers— and highly susceptible to unemployment and low wages. But within the same occupational class—and usually even within the same occupation—a woman receives only one-third to two-thirds of a man's pay. Since 1939, the dollar increases in women's salaries and wages have lagged significantly behind those of men.[39] In 1939, women headed or constituted 20 per cent of the families and individuals in the lowest income-fifth; by 1947, it was 30 per cent, and by 1956, it was 35 per cent.[40]

A good deal of attention is being directed nowadays to the sociological impact of another trend that has also been producing economic repercussions—the rising number of youthful marriages and the consequent formation of families when earnings are still low. The median age of marriage for men dropped from 24.3 years in 1940 to 22.3 years in 1956. For women, the corresponding median ages were 21.5 years and 20.2 years.[41] These changes in the divorce rate and age of marriage, as well as the general economic position of women, have compensated for the movement of many workers out of the poverty class because of rising real income.

REGION, RACE, AND INCOME

There are other important determinants of income, although it must be kept in mind that occupation and age are the two most important and consistent ones. Regions account for substantial variations in income. However, since 1920, there has been a steady leveling off of such differences. Since 1950, population has been growing fastest in the North Central and, especially, Western states—regions with per-capita incomes close to the national average.[42] The most rapid increase in state per-capita incomes since 1929 has occurred in the South, even though they are still well below the national average. In the rural areas, the South accounts for almost 60 per cent of families earning less than $2,000 a year, but in large cities, suburbs, and small cities, the differences between the North or West and the South are much less significant. In fact, the South had a smaller percentage of urban consumer units in the $0–$1,000 income class in 1954 than the West.[43]

The low income of the Negro is a major factor in the anatomy of poverty in the South and in the United States. The Negro's economic position compared to the white's improved sharply from 1939 to 1947, primarily due to the end of unemployment, which hits the Negro harder. In 1947, the Negro male's annual median wage was 54 per cent of the white's; ten years later, that figure was 1 per cent higher—or virtually no change at all. And despite the highly touted shift upward in Negro occupations, which presumably would produce higher incomes, the segment of Negro men who were unskilled or service workers dropped only from 56 per cent to 52 per cent in the twenty-year span from 1940 to 1959.[44]

It is still a rule of thumb that the number of Negroes in the lowest-income classes and in poverty situations is twice the number of whites. In 1950, Negroes, representing 9.4 per cent of the urban population, constituted 15.8 per cent of the $0–$1,000 urban consumer units and 21.1 per cent of the $1,000–$2,000 units. Similarly, in 1954, Southern Negro farmers constituted one-tenth of the nation's farm families, but one-fifth of the farmers in the $0–$1,000 income class.[45] In early 1958, the unemployment rate among Negroes was 12 per cent, compared to 6 per cent among whites.

Now let us think in terms of the future. In the 1950's, the rate of growth of the Negro population was two-thirds greater than that of the white population. Thus, the proportionate number of Negroes is rising. And since their economic position is not, the logical expectation is for a continuation and expansion of Negro low-income and poverty groups.

Nevertheless, it should not be thought that income inequality is primarily a racial problem, for the overwhelming majority of the low-paid are white. Their economic position is due to factors that are far more difficult to cope with than racial discrimination. The vested interests in income in-equality, and the economic fabric that supports that inequal-ity, are very much stronger than any opposition to better job opportunities for Negroes.

THE RELIEF ROLLS

A measure of the economic pressures since the Depression of the 1930's can be found in statistics on relief. In 1935–36, 1.5 million individuals and 4.5 million families—or roughly 20 million people—received some form of relief, however short the duration or small the amount.[46] At any one time probably no more than 12 million, and possibly far fewer, were on relief. These included a hard core of permanent recipients and a much larger group of unemployed who were willing and able to work.

In February, 1958, 6.6 million people were receiving relief. The recession deepened, and by May, 1958, the number had jumped to 7.1 million, the increase consisting almost wholly of unemployed workers who had exhausted their unemploy-ment compensation or who were not covered by it.[47] Of the total number receiving relief in February, 2.5 million were over sixty-five and unable to live on social-insurance benefits, and 400,000 were blind or disabled. Another 2.6 million were receiving aid to dependent children (only one-fifth of these, contrary to common opinion, were illegitimate).[48] Most of the remainder of those on relief were unemployed workers. The 6.6 million on relief in February, 1958, is substantially smaller than the 20 million in 1935–36, although if all per-sons who were on relief at any time in 1957–58 were included, the difference would undoubtedly shrink.

Since the early 1950's, most of the increase in relief cases can be attributed to recession-caused unemployment. Mich-igan, for example, heavily hit by unemployment in the reces-sion of 1958, raised its relief outlay for 1958 to two and one-half times the 1957 figure. In Illinois, Pennsylvania, Connecticut, Ohio, and New York, general relief rolls doubled and tripled with the addition of unemployed workers who had run out of unemployment checks or were ineligible for them. Even after the restoration of industrial output, a disturbingly large number of the unemployed were not recalled to work.[49] The applauders of the economy have ignored the fact that "insular poverty" exists in many states besides West Virginia, and that relief, with all its humiliating impact on its recipients, is still very much a part of the contemporary economic picture. Few analysts of the American society have conceded the significance of the continuation of relief in recent years.

6

The Extent of Poverty

To what extent have these factors leading to poverty
counterbalanced the real-income gains of many American
occupations? The answer is of major importance, since it will
indicate the degree to which the American economy, with its
great inequality of income, has created a class of families
and individuals living in poverty or below the minimum
levels for health and decency.

A number of Government studies have analyzed the cost
of what has been variously called the "American," the "minimum health and decency," and—the term I will use—the
"maintenance" standard of living. The most reliable of
these was made in 1935 by the Works Progress Administration, and it, along with those made by the Department of
Agriculture and the National Resources Committee, constitutes the essential basis of the postwar Bureau of Labor
Statistics estimates of the cost of a "maintenance" budget.

The maintenance budget is a synthesis of what families
actually spend, modified to include what they must have to
meet minimum health criteria. It is *not* a relative or changing
standard such as that employed by "social workers [who]
will call a person 'underprivileged' whose scale of living is
considerably below the average."[1] The level this budget
describes is a "threshold," or "breaking point."

"This budget," explains the Bureau of Labor Statistics,
"does not approach the content of what may be considered

a satisfactory American standard of living, nor does its cost measure what families in this country would have to spend to secure the 'abundant life.' " In such a more elevated scheme, "provision would be made for future education of the children and for economic security through saving. These and other desirable improvements above a maintenance level of living would require annual disbursements considerably in excess of the money values of the budget used in this investigation."[2]

In another study, the Bureau says that "this level of living represents essentially a breaking point in our society. It divides the population into two groups, the lower of which is struggling to attain a physically more adequate existence. It is only above this level that people have enough to begin to think largely in terms of the quality of their living."[3] A third Bureau report continues this thought: "Study of these data shows that at the lower end of the income scale differences in purchases by families at successive income levels are primarily in the quantities of items bought; in the higher-income brackets these differences are due to the choice of higher quality and more expensive items."[4]

The WPA study also calculated an "emergency" budget, which cost about 70 per cent as much as the maintenance budget. It warned that "those forced to exist at the emergency level for an extended period may be subjected to serious health hazards."[5] Below this line, it is clear, the family or individual lives in poverty, and expenditures are guided, not by social norms of well-being, but by the demands of survival.

The WPA's maintenance budget, compiled in 1935, is itemized in very great detail. The budget is calculated for a worker's family, of four people, in an urban area, with the wife unemployed, but cost adjustments are possible for families of different sizes. For example, a family of two requires only 65 per cent of the basic budget, a family of three needs only 84 per cent, a family of five needs 115 per cent, and a family of six needs 129 per cent.[6] The home is assumed to be a rented four- or five-room apartment or house in fair repair, with plumbing, private toilet, gas, and electricity. No allocation is made for savings other than a small insurance policy.

The postwar Bureau of Labor Statistics budgets, calculated to "maintain a level of adequate living according to prewar standards prevailing in the large cities of the United States," are similar in most major items.[7] The family sees fewer movies but buys more magazines. The one change of consequence is the addition of a car six to nine years old for 74 per cent of the families living in cities of from 50,000 to 1.9 million and for 40 per cent of the families in larger cities. In both instances, allowance is made for the purchase of a new car every 12 to 18 years. Three members of the family see a movie once every three weeks, and one member sees a movie once every two weeks. There is no telephone in the house, but the family makes three pay calls a week. They buy one book a year and write one letter a week.

The father buys one heavy wool suit every two years and a light wool suit every three years; the wife, one suit every ten years or one skirt every five years. Every three or four years, depending on the distance and time involved, the family takes a vacation outside their own city. In 1950, the family spent a total of $80 to $90 on all types of home furnishings, electrical appliances, and laundry equipment. Naturally, the mother does all cleaning, cooking, and laundry. The family eats cheaper cuts of meat several times a week, but has more expensive cuts on holidays. The entire family consumes a total of two five-cent ice-cream cones, one five-cent candy bar, two bottles of soda, and one bottle of beer a week. The family owes no money, but has no savings except for a small insurance policy, and presumably no fear.[8]

To maintain this level for a family of four required an

average of $3,300 in 1947, $3,717 in 1950, and $4,166 in 1951, the last year in which official data were released. It is possible to bring this figure up to date by adjusting the BLS data for the increase in the Consumer Price Index, but this is not completely satisfactory. The maintenance budget is based on a somewhat different existence, and a mere financial updating would understate the true cost of a 1961 equivalent by at least several hundred dollars.

A number of private budget estimates are also available, the most reliable being that of the Heller Committee of the University of California. This budget, which includes everything that 50 per cent or more of American families buy or own, requires for city dwellers an income about one-quarter greater than needed for the BLS budget.[9]

Estimates on the population percentages living at various consumption levels, each defined by the author, were made before 1935 without the aid of reliable statistics. Newel Howland Comish, in *The Standard of Living*, estimated that in 1910, 17 per cent of American families lived on the "pauper standard," 35 per cent on the "minimum-of-subsistence standard," 44 per cent on the "health-and-comfort standard," and 4 per cent on the "luxury standard."[10] Comish's definitions and data were at best speculative. A decade later, Charles S. Wyand, defining the "comfort" standard as that point at which a family's outlay for "sundries" exceeded a quarter of its income, estimated that in 1929 only 34 per cent of the nonfarm and 11 per cent of the farm families achieved this standard.[11] The Brookings Institution, in the best estimate for the pre-1935 period, calculated that in 1929, 42 per cent of the consumer units lived at or below the "subsistence-and-poverty level" and another 36 per cent lived at least at the "minimum-comfort" level.[12]

In 1935–36, 49 per cent of families and unrelated individuals lived below the "maintenance" standard set by the WPA, and 28 per cent were below the "emergency" standard, set at 70 per cent of the maintenance level. The 1935–36 maintenance standard excluded car, electric refrigerator, gas stove, washing machine, and a few small appliances, though the allocation for these in the post-World War II budget is very small.

These estimates are far from ideal, however, since to calculate the percentage of families and unrelated individuals living below certain standards, we need specific data that did not exist in any form prior to 1939. First, there is a need for a precise, accurate, and constant definition of poverty and of minimum-decency standards and their cost. This we now have in rough form for 1935–36 (the WPA study) and for most postwar years (the BLS budgets). Second, there must be detailed information on the distribution of family sizes among the various income classes so that the percentages of spending units living below the maintenance or emergency income, adjusted for family size, can be calculated. Such data are now available. Thus, it is now a relatively simple task to calculate accurately the national percentage of families and unattached individuals living below maintenance and emergency levels from 1947 on.

Before a national analysis can be made, however, certain items should be noted. The maintenance standard costs less in a rural area, primarily to the extent that food is obtained as income-in-kind or purchased more cheaply. As the data in Chapter 1 show, the importance of such income-in-kind among farmers has declined rapidly since World War II. This is reflected in the fact that in 1941, the maintenance standard cost 27 per cent more in urban areas than in rural; in 1945, the urban maintenance standard cost only 18 per cent more.[13] It is most likely that this price distinction has continued to decline rapidly. Differences in clothing expenditures between urban and rural families are comparatively minor.[14] Income-in-kind is not included in the following calculations, but it is relatively inconsequential among poor urban families. More important, the debts or credit available to lower-income groups are omitted. All that is shown is the standard of living available to families and unattached individuals on the basis of their total money income. It is a close approximation of actual American living standards, not an exact reproduction. But, at worst, it is far more accurate than the speculations based on ignorance that have been so prominent in this area.

Since 1947, one-half of the nation's families and unattached individuals have had an income too small to provide them with a maintenance standard of living, and one-third have had an income too small to provide even an emergency standard of living. The seeming drop between 1951 and 1957 in the percentage of families and unattached individuals below these levels is due primarily to the fact that the Bureau of Labor Statistics ceased collecting data for calculations after 1951, and the only available statistics are somewhat less comprehensive (see Table IX).

TABLE IX

PERCENTAGE OF NATIONAL SPENDING UNITS BELOW
MAINTENANCE AND EMERGENCY INCOME LEVELS [15]

Number in Spending Unit	Below Maintenance			Below Emergency		
	1947	1951	1957	1947	1951	1957
1	11.9	11.7	11.9	9.6	8.5	9.6
2	10.8	12.2	9.9	7.5	8.4	6.5
3	9.0	8.6	5.3	5.2	5.0	2.9
4	8.0	8.2	5.5	4.2	4.2	2.3
5	5.0	5.4	4.7	2.7	2.8	2.1
6	3.0	3.1	3.2	1.9	2.1	1.7
7-plus	3.5	3.2	3.5	2.4	2.4	2.4
Total of all units	51.2	52.4	44.0	33.5	33.4	27.5

Here is the significant conclusion that emerges from these figures: *The gains of relatively full employment and a normally ascending real income have been largely offset by the rise of new causes of poverty and by the perpetuation of an important segment of the traditional causes.*

This finding is of crucial importance in the face of the steady growth of the newer causes of poverty. It can indicate only a long-term continuation of poverty and near-poverty. Above all, it is a condemnation of the American economy for its failure to solve the fundamental social and economic problems of both the present and the future.

Below the emergency standard of living, there clearly exists a state of poverty. Between the emergency and maintenance standards, there exists a shadowy area ranging from poverty to hard-pressed insecurity. Unattached individuals, a segment that is heavily weighted with persons sixty-five years old and older, are disproportionately represented in these areas. And more than two-thirds of all families with six or more members have been below the maintenance level since 1947.

There is a direct relationship between family size and failure to earn a maintenance or emergency income: As the family size increases, so does the incidence of inadequate income. In 1951, for example, 44 per cent of all two-person families earned less than the maintenance standard, as opposed to 77 per cent of all families of seven or more.

Several independent analyses of the people below the maintenance level have appeared since Table IX was published in preliminary form, and these reinforce my conclusions. The first summarized the major (and as yet unpublished) findings of the New York State Interdepartmental Committee on Low Incomes study of poverty in 1949. It was based on the public and private welfare-agency 'standard budget," which was slightly lower in cost than the BLS budget. In 1949, the study found, after the necessary adjustments for family size, 30 per cent of all families and 50 per cent of all unrelated individuals in the state of New York had incomes below the standard budget.[16] Since New York had the fourth-highest per-capita income of all the states, the extent of poverty was doubtless substantially greater in most of the 44 other states.

Another analysis concerned couples and single persons aged sixty-five and over who lived by themselves. It set out to determine what percentage of them were living below a "total standard" budget, which was approximately equivalent to the emergency level used in my study. According to this estimate, made by economists Peter O. Steiner and Robert Dorfman in *The Economic Status of the Aged* (1957), 45–50 per cent of the couples, 52–58 per cent of the unattached men, and 71–75 per cent of the unattached women had incomes below this standard.

In a study of families in large cities in the relatively prosperous North Central and Northeast regions of the United States, Eleanor M. Snyder, an economist, concluded that in 1950, 46.3 per cent of them lived at a "low economic status" that was not "adequate."[17]

In 1939, of the 94 clerical, sales, skilled, semiskilled, service, and unskilled occupations employing men and listed in the Census data on *average* annual incomes, 63 paid less than the $1,333 required to support a BLS maintenance standard for four, and 35 paid less than the emergency level for four. In 1949, 84 of these 94 occupations paid less than the $3,608 necessary to meet the maintenance standard and 55 occupations paid less than the emergency level for four.[18]

WORKING WIVES AND CREDIT

The rise of working wives—from 15 per cent of married women in 1940 to 28 per cent in 1955—can be interpreted as both a cause of prosperity and a sign of distress during inflation.[19] All earlier discussions in terms of spending units or consumer units include the earnings of wives in unit incomes. Most working wives do not earn a great deal, but whatever they receive is generally enough to move the family up the income scale a class or two. In 1956, the average American working wife earned $1,300, and a somewhat larger percentage of families with working wives than of those without were in the $4,000–$10,000 income bracket.[20]

More than one-third of the working wives were married to skilled or semiskilled workers, and the incidence of working wives was the highest in these classes—which in large part accounts for much of their seeming prosperity.[21] Without this army of working wives, the number of families living below the maintenance and emergency levels would be much greater. Wives of blue-collar workers enter the labor force primarily because they have large families that cannot be adequately supported on their husbands' earnings, and in late 1960, 1 million wives of unemployed men were the sole breadwinners of their families. In the $10,000-plus income class in 1950, the per-capita income of the few blue-collar families was less than one-half that of families of clerical workers and not quite one-third that of families of self-employed persons.[22] The heads of these blue-collar families earned less than half the family income, their prosperity being due mostly to working wives and children.

Another, generally unnoticed, cause of the recent comparative prosperity has been the rise of "moonlighting"—the holding of a second, and even a third job. Among men and unmarried women who were already employed, 4.8 per cent, or more than 3 million, were moonlighters in 1958, as contrasted to only 2.9 per cent in 1950. In Akron, Ohio, where the rubber companies have had a six-hour day for three decades, as high as 50 per cent of the rubber workers hold two jobs; 10 per cent of them have two full-time jobs in rubber plants. Although moonlighting may be a cause of prosperity, it is also a result of legitimate anxieties felt by many workers in an economy that threatens periodic layoffs and technological unemployment.[23]

The rise of consumer installment credit is one of the most important keys to understanding increases in the nation's standard of living since World War II. Outstanding installment credit amounted to 3.7 per cent of national personal income in 1929, 4.5 per cent in 1935, and 3.5 per cent of national personal income in 1947; it rose to 9.9 per cent in 1957.[24]

Installment credit since World War II has made possible a maintenance standard of living for an unknown, doubtless significant portion of the American people. As a general practice, the annual volume of installment buying exceeds the repayment volume. The gap between consumption and repayment may be considered an addition to income. Thus, the debt margin after repayments added only 1.4 per cent to personal income in 1952, a peak 1.7 per cent in 1955, and a mere 0.6 per cent in 1957—an average of 1.1 per cent in 1946–57. In 1935–36, this debt added only 0.9 per cent, but only about one-fifth of all families utilized installment credit, as opposed to about one-half of all spending units in the 1950's.[25] This indicates that for families utilizing credit, installment buying has been of only minor consequence to their economic position.

The incidence of installment debt is closely related to income. The peak incidence occurs in the classes closest to the BLS maintenance level, which are probably most conscious of their economic life. In early 1960, 25 per cent of those in the $0–$2,000 class, 60 per cent of those in the $5,000–$7,500, and 46 per cent of those in the $10,000-and-over class had some installment debt.[26] The low-income spending units going into debt are much more likely to commit a very large portion of their income—40 per cent or more—to installment payments. In the much more numerous quarter of spending units that pledged 10 to 39 per cent of their incomes in 1960 to meet payments, the middle-income classes predominate.[27]

When one considers all forms of consumer debt—install- ment, real estate, loans, charge accounts, etc.—extensive obligations are the rule for most spending units. And the lowest income-tenth is by far the most committed in relation to income, a reflection of its need to exploit credit in order to keep body and soul together. In 1939 and 1950, the total national consumer debt amounted to 32 per cent of the annual personal income, but by 1959, it had risen to 51 per cent. For the lowest income-tenth, it was a very exceptional 160 per cent in 1950.[28]

Installment credit adds comparatively little to the purchas- ing power of Americans as a whole when repayments are taken into account. Its growing percentage of personal in- come only weakens the economy by allowing people to con- sume now on the basis of a future that is always unpredict- able. It represents a mortgage on future income that must eventually require a reduction in future expenditures if real income fails to rise. A worker who is laid off or put on a shorter work week must curtail current spending in order to pay for past installment purchases. During the recession in the first half of 1958, as in early 1954, Americans sharply cut back on new installment debts, thereby reducing sales and, ultimately, employment. At the same time, repossessions for nonpayment were nearly double those for the first half of 1957. In the 1954 recession, the proportion of finance- company loans contracted to repay overdue debts increased to 33 per cent, as opposed to 10 per cent in 1945. Such loans, of course, only compound the chances of consumer miscal- culation of future income.

The instability of installment purchases is primarily due to changes in consumer real income, not Keynesian manipula- tion of the interest rate, and as Avram Kisselgoff has asserted, there is "little promise that cyclical fluctuations in consumer expenditures can be greatly influenced solely by changes in credit terms."[29] The judgment of the Federal Reserve Board in its neglected 1957 study is less reserved:

Major depressions preceding World War II were characterized by debt defaults and related difficulties. What started out to be a relatively modest problem of financial adjustment sometimes turned out to have vastly multiplied effects. . . . Even if a relatively modest proportion of borrowing consumers defaulted on obligations having a large average size and a slim margin of collateral protection, lending institutions could conceivably raise their lending standards so sharply that the volume of new business would be greatly reduced. A spiral of debt liquidation could even be started. The cyclical effects of such a development are self-evident. . . .

Safety margins depend on the equity of consumers in what they own, the price stability or instability of their . . . liquid assets, and the stability of their incomes. All forms of credit . . . have this in common: they make it possible for individual economic units to spend out of phase with income. But the income of the borrower, whether business or consumer, must continue to be large enough to cover repayments or he will be in default. . . . Even though the analogy of 1929 is of diminishing relevance, the possibility of an episode of drastic and spiraling liquidation should not be dismissed.[30]

CONCLUSION

Since social status eventually becomes equal to economic position, and since major differences exist in the economic positions of the occupational classes, there is little empirical support for the assertion by Lipset, Riesman, and numerous others that America, in terms of economic and social status, is becoming a middle-class society. The income gaps between unskilled, semiskilled, and skilled workers have remained fairly stable, at least since 1939, and their apparent advance in relation to clerical and sales workers reflects more the economic decline of this white-collar class in an inflationary economy than the ascent of the blue-collar workers. The stability of the blue-collar workers in their various income-tenths has been sufficiently constant to suggest that plumbers and janitors, for example, are not moving toward the economic elite. The real income of many workers has increased at a rate similar to that of the 1920's, and this is primarily due to improved economic conditions resulting from World War II. Many, however, still receive an income too small to maintain a decent standard of living, and many still undergo periodic unemployment.

The significant major changes in occupational groupings are occurring in the clerical and sales class. Two trends are at work: An increasing segment of this class is being economically "massified" at a low-income level, and this class as a whole is experiencing the greatest growth of any class.[31] Contrary to the general assumption, its expansion is not resulting in a corresponding growth in the "middle" economic class. Instead, it is swelling the low-income brackets.

This dynamic element of growth exists in other new causes of poverty—such as the mounting percentage of aged people and the rising number of women heading households. These trends have combined with the still-important traditional causes of poverty—low wages, unemployment, and the like—to preserve the proportion of submaintenance poverty in the United States. The highly touted "welfare state" measures, consisting of penurious minimum-wage laws, shabby old-age benefits, and inadequate unemployment compensation, have not significantly counterbalanced the growth and strength of the forces of poverty.

The poor remain and will likely increase in number in the near future. The predominantly prosperous middle-class society is only an image in the minds of isolated academicians.

These new causes of poverty are sociological in nature and

economic in consequence, and they are a major new aspect of the American social structure and a basic problem for social policy. If, for any reason, consumption fails to keep up with technological innovations and productive capacity, the shock of resulting economic crises can have an economic impact on important elements of the population that are relatively "normal" sociologically.

For some, however, there is an element of consolation derived from the concept that such poverty, as Joseph J. Spengler claims, is "due largely to permanent causes." This notion is certainly relevant to evaluating the economy, for if it can be shown that the poor are responsible for poverty— or at least that the existing economic system is not—then the conservative implications for social analysis and policy are all too apparent. However, this line of thought is less plausible than it might seem. The late Joseph Schumpeter has pointed to the significance of the rationalization of all life in a capitalist economy in forcing the disintegration of the family and its economic values.[32] The low economic status of the Negroes, it must be noted, could be radically changed in short order if the 2,000 or so men who control the major American corporations really desired such changes. The worker who deserts his family in a period of unemployment may have a streak of the devil in him, but he more than likely cannot feed them and this, too, is a factor of consequence. The economically depressed position of the aged reflects the inability or the unwillingness of the status quo to meet adequately the changing circumstances that should, ideally, be solved as a normal consequence of living in a modern technology guided by rational and democratic values.

There is no consolation to the submaintenance poor in any of these explanations. It is a most dismaying fact that in contemporary America, the aged generally end their lives in a condition of economic want of the barest sort. For those of all ages living below the maintenance level, there is no ability to live or act beyond boundaries not calculated to satisfy very immediate and basic needs. There are the constant fear and anxiety of economic insecurity and the overwhelming limitations on opportunities for freely developing creative, independent lives.

7

Income Inequality and Consumption

Inequality of income is not an abstraction that has no effect on the day-to-day existence of people. It permeates every aspect of the lives of the American populace—poor and rich alike. Translated into consumption, it creates a visible class structure that determines the immediate existence as well as the longer-range life opportunities of each income class—from tonight's supper to the school a child will, or will not, attend.

Despite this reality, the theme of America as a relatively classless society is fundamental in the writings of many social scientists, who assume that consumption and the distribution of economic-status symbols have been equalized. "The relative equality in the distribution of a very large national income implies that the differences between classes are moderate rather than intense," write Seymour M. Lipset and Reinhard Bendix.[1] This equality has "permitted many persons, especially urban industrial workers, to indulge in 'conspicuous consumption' to a greater degree than ever before," according to Gideon Sjoberg.[2] "One need not indulge in flights of fancy," suggests Kurt Mayer, "to see that middle-class patterns of consumption are spreading rapidly among manual workers in the United States," resulting in an "assimilation of life styles."[3]

This pattern of increasingly equalized consumption, and the means by which it is shaped, are the central ideas in David Riesman's *The Lonely Crowd*. We live in an "age of consumption" rather than an "age of production," and this is possible largely because the "means of consumption are widely distributed." "Most people in America today—the 'overprivileged' two-thirds, let us say, as against the underprivileged third—can afford to attend to, and allow their characters to be shaped by, situational differences of a subtler nature than those arising from bare economic necessity and their relations to the means of production."[4] Class differences, Riesman says, are more likely to be expressed in the manner of consumption than in the item itself. Because the psychological advantages of conspicuous consumption are reduced in a society of abundance in which most can duplicate the performance, we consume "inconspicuously," Riesman observes.

But is it true that consumption has been equalized even though, as I have demonstrated, distribution of income has not? Does our higher level of real income within the same framework of inequality allow most income classes to possess the symbols of high economic status and the products of economic abundance? (Since the income-to-savings ratio of the top income class has not changed markedly in recent decades, we can exclude the possibility that the top income classes have cut the percentage of their income devoted to consumption expenditures.)

In answering these questions, I will attempt to illustrate the equality or inequality of consumption in a number of crucial areas. First, and perhaps most important of all, is higher education, which involves the utilization of talents. Also of great importance is medical care, which concerns distribution of health. Next is housing, a fundamental index to well-being. The last area is the automobile, seen as a basic status symbol rather than a necessity, and we will examine the common belief, expressed by Talcott Parsons, that "many very high-status people drive Fords and Chevrolets (and some not-so-high drive Cadillacs). . . ."

Finally, the pattern of over-all consumption by income class will be examined and related to income inequality.

EDUCATION. THE LOST GENERATIONS

Education is not merely an article of consumption; it is the major channel of interclass mobility and the door to opportunity.

It can be argued that inequality in education reflects, not inequality in income, but inequality in the distribution of talents among income and occupational classes. If this is so, the distribution of income may follow the distribution of individual talents and inherent worth. Joseph J. Spengler sets forth this line of reasoning: "In a society marked by considerable ability inequality and by high specificity of tasks requiring to be performed, the allocation of positions and hence of income will be dominated by achievement. . . ."[5] It is possible to test the validity of this proposition by examining the extent and location of unutilized talent in our society and the distribution of IQ's by occupational classes.

Low education has generally been presented as a cause of low income, not an effect. Casting it in the role of cause has generally reinforced the upper-class disdain for the masses and supported the rationale that the income distribution is based, ultimately, on an unequal distribution of intelligence. Economic mobility in a technology and society enormously—and increasingly—dependent on the formally trained expert ultimately reflects the extent of equality in education. In estimating inequality of consumption and the degree to which economic mobility reflects income distribution, it is obviously important to determine whether educational opportunity is concentrated in the same manner as income.

Intelligence tests are at best a debatable means for measuring the distribution of intelligence. Distractions, day-to-day variations in individual performance or ability to concentrate, and similar factors create a significant margin of error. Further, psychologist John B. Miner declares in his important study *Intelligence in the United States* (1957), "intelligence tests do not in any sense tap native, inherent capacities."[6] Such tests are weighted, in varying degrees, to stress verbal understanding and to underplay mechanical, spatial, and numerical comprehension. Verbal ability, of course, is clearly important in communication, but in many areas of modern life, especially in technology and science, it is only one of many factors necessary for achievement. Also, vocabulary is in large part a result of parental background and class environment. The premium placed on education by the middle class (the higher-income white-collar workers, professionals, and managers) maximizes the extent to which their children are given superior preparation in verbal skills. The desire for attention and success is often more important to school achievement than mental capacity, and this is clearly a middle-class attribute.

But let us suppose now that IQ scores do provide an accurate index to the ability to utilize education. On that basis, we must conclude that a college education—the successful exploitation of an IQ rating—is primarily a reflection of income class. It is estimated that the top quarter of the IQ-ranked population, those scoring 110 and over, can attend college profitably. Of these, 40 per cent graduate from high school and go on to college—but another 20 per cent do not even complete high school. Of the top 16 per cent by IQ, those scoring 120 and over, only one-half enter college and only one-third graduate.[7]

There can be little doubt that children of the upper-income classes are given the best and most extensive higher educations. An expert on the economics of education, Coleman R. Griffith, asserted in 1951 that "the ablest young folks from the highest occupational income groups have about a four to one advantage over the ablest youth in the lower group in getting to college. If differences in ability are left out of account, the odds come out ten to one in favor of children from the higher income groups."[8] Similar patterns have been consistently established in succeeding studies.

The economic factor can easily be seen in these results of a 1957 survey of top-IQ high-school graduates who planned to attend college: Those who went had an average of 1.9 children in their family, and those who did not go had an average of 2.8.[9] In 1955, 18 per cent of the families had 54 per cent of the children, and it is probable that college education is out of the question for them unless they are in the highest income classes.[10] The poorest 66 per cent of the spending units, those earning less than $4,000, supplied only 35 per cent of the college students in 1952; the top income-tenth supplied 31 per cent. The poorer half of the nation provided only 15 per cent of the students in private colleges in 1959, and 30 per cent in public. Family support is decisive, accounting for about 60 per cent of student income. Student earnings amounted to only one-quarter of the total, and scholarships for about 5 per cent.[11]

Our knowledge of the distribution of IQ by occupation and the extent of unexploited talent suggests that unexploited talent is to be found primarily in children of fathers in low-income occupations. From the blue-collar class come about one-half the children in the top IQ quarter, which is in proportion to their share of the children.[12] But only 26 per cent of their children who graduate from high school go on to college, and only 15 per cent graduate from college. Among children of professional men, the corresponding figures are 67 and 40 per cent.[13] According to Miner's study, "at least 66.6 per cent of all workers have the intellectual potential for jobs at a higher level than that at which they are presently employed."[14]

One thing is certain; the thesis that distribution of income reflects distribution of intelligence has no factual basis.

Obviously, a family earning $3,000 a year cannot significantly help their child to obtain a university education. But if he can attend a state or municipal school in his area and he will take on the handicap of earning his expenses, having only a limited time for study, and perhaps stretching his studies out beyond four years, he can get a bachelor's degree. Most students from low-income families obtain their degrees in just this undesirable manner. However, such a basis practically rules out graduate or professional study.

In 1952, the average college student from a $0–$3,000 family spent about half as much on his education as the student from a $15,000-plus family.[15] This difference was reflected in the quality of education, the first-rate educations being reserved for the children of the economic elite. The student from the lower-income family is likely to be a commuter and to major in education or industrial management rather than law, medicine, or the liberal arts. He is much more likely to be a student at a municipal university than at an Ivy League college.[16] In 1948, the nonscholarship student in Harvard's class of 1951, for example, came from a home with a median income nearly five times the national average; also, 81 per cent of the class were sons of professionals or top managerial personnel, while a mere 6 per cent were sons of blue-collar workers.[17]

The student from a low-income background who manages to go to college will enter an occupational class of higher status than this father's, but not having a first-rate education will seriously impede his social and economic mobility.

Scholarship aid, amounting to only 5 per cent of the total student costs, does comparatively little to make a higher education accessible to the lower-income potential student. If he cannot finance the major part of his expenses—an increasingly difficult task given the doubling of tuition costs in private schools over the past decade—he will probably not enter school, even though most high-IQ high-school graduates who do not enter college would be willing to do so if their expenses were paid.[18] Much of the existing scholarship aid goes to children of middle- and high-income earners—an inevitable concentration, because five private universities have received nearly one-half of all endowment funds since the 1920's. Only 3 per cent of all colleges controlled one-third of the scholarship funds, and one-fifth of the colleges accounted for nearly two-thirds of the scholarship funds in 1959.

In 1952–53, 35 per cent of all scholarship aid went to students from families earning $5,000–$11,000, and 14 per cent went to students from the $11,000-plus income class.[19] In 1957, slightly more than one-half the scholarship applicants in a large group of colleges were the children of professionals and managers, and only one in ten came from the $0–$3,000 class.[20] Scholarship aid, in large part, goes to educate children of the lower-income members of the professional and managerial classes, and does comparatively little to increase the mobility between occupational classes. This is especially true of the elite colleges. In 1959, the average scholarship student in three Ivy League schools came from a home with an income of more than $7,000. As the associate director of admissions at Harvard, Richard G. King, confessed in 1957: "The extremely needy student tends to get helped if he can reduce his need by commuting or if he is so able, active, and personable as to stand head and shoulders above his competitors. If he is just 'very good' we send him an admission certificate, deny him a scholarship, let him go to college locally and become more of a success than his father, and then wait to award a smaller scholarship to *his* children in the *next* generation."[21]

HEALTH AND INCOME

Inequality in medical care is a problem of different magnitude from that of inequality in overt economic-status symbols. A car may confer prestige, but medical care can extend longevity, reduce the incidence of illness, and perhaps mean the difference between life and death. The significance of medical care can be expressed only very partially and inadequately in statistical terms, for suffering, deprivation, and personal tragedy can never be measured quantitatively.

The average member of the $10,000-plus income class spends twice as much on his per-capita medical care as the average member of the $0–$4,000 classes. This inequality is modified to the extent that within any income class the sixty-five-year-and-over group spends more of its income on medical care; but within any age group, the inequalities in medical-care expenditures reflect income.[22] This inequality is evidenced in the number of visits to doctors and the number and duration of treated illnesses. One study of the level of health in Michigan in 1948 showed that 45 per cent of the persons in the $0–$1,000 class, as compared to 10 per cent in the $5,000-plus class, had untreated positive symptoms of illness.[23] In 1953, 17 per cent of those in the $0–$2,000 class, as contrasted to 56 per cent in the $7,500-and-over class, consulted a dentist. The quality of the care varied as greatly as the incidence of visits.[24]

Various types of health insurance now cover over two-thirds of the American population, but in 1959, all forms of health insurance paid for only 24 per cent of the nation's personal medical expenses. Yet even this inadequate insurance was available in 1953 to only 41 per cent of those earning $0–$3,000, compared to 80 per cent of those in the $5,000-plus class. Nearly two-thirds of the persons sixty-five and over did not have hospital insurance in 1958.[25] Among lower-income families having such insurance, reduced coverage was the rule. Since the personal medical debt is concentrated in a small proportion of the population—in 1953, 11 per cent of the families had 43 per cent of the medical debt—the inadequacy of health insurance, with its limited liability, should surprise no one. Even moderate illness can mean financial catastrophe to most American families, especially when combined with loss of earnings. In 1953, 7 per cent of American families incurred medical debts amounting to more than 20 per cent of their annual income; 2 per cent incurred debts amounting to more than 50 per cent of their annual income; 1 per cent incurred debts amounting to more than their annual income.[26] The effect of such expenses on most families is enormous, and as a result, low- and middle-income families often avoid medical treatment as long as possible. The consequences are reflected in the higher incidence of disease and illness among these income classes, compared to the lower incidence among the wealthy.

Research into the incidence of illness by income class since World War II has been unsystematic, and not comparable in depth and scope to the national health studies of 1928–31 and 1935–36. Both these studies reached the identical conclusion: Very low income is directly related to illness and undoubtedly a major cause. This was true both of infectious diseases, such as tuberculosis and the like, and degenerative diseases, such as cardiovascular and kidney diseases, and cancer. In 1935–36, for example, the per-capita disability in five nonrelief income classes was radically lower than that in the relief class. Compared with the incidence in the $3,000-plus class, the under-$1,000 class had 335 per cent more hernia, 292 per cent more tuberculosis, 212 per cent more blindness and deafness, 102 per cent more rheumatism, 48 per cent more cancer, 112 per cent more nervous and mental diseases, and 131 per cent more diabetes. The relative incidence of illness in the relief group was even larger. Within the same age group in 1928–31, disabling illnesses of all sorts were about twice as great in the lowest nonrelief income class as in the highest.[27]

Recent data are very sparse. In a 1949–51 study of the white population of Houston, Texas, John M. Ellis examined the mortality rates of certain diseases among five major income classes. He found that, compared to the highest income class, the lowest had a rate six times as great for tuberculosis, one-third greater for heart diseases, and one-fifth greater for nephritis. In 1960, an ethical-drug firm reported that such supposed illnesses of the rich as ulcers, hypertension, and arteriosclerosis are found more frequently among workers than among executives.[28]

Fortunately, we have considerably more information about recent correlations between income and mental illness. Robert E. Clark, in his 1949 study of Chicago mental hospitals, found that skilled workers are five times more likely to be hospitalized for psychoses than are professionals or managerial personnel. Semiskilled and unskilled workers are more than six times more likely. August B. Hollingshead and Fredrick C. Redlich, in their major study *Social Class and Mental Illness* (1958), classify the incidence of psychoses according to the five classes of Lloyd Warner's "index of social position," in which income is an important but by no means the exclusive component. They found that in New Haven, Connecticut, the community utilized for study, the rate of treated psychiatric illness per 100,000 persons was three times greater in Class V, the poorest class, than in Classes I and II. Treatment for Class V psychotics had been far inferior and cheaper than the treatment for Class I and Class II psychotics, which had cost three times as much.[29] The differences in mental treatment for the poor and for the rich is the difference between the analyst's couch and Bedlam.

The poorer medical facilities for the lower-income ill compound their suffering. City hospitals are often vast, impersonal institutions that increase the likelihood of inadequate treatment and unnecessary death. These hospitals, plus dental-school clinics often staffed by novices, surround illness for the poor with additional uncalled-for horrors that statistics can never capture.

HOUSING AND INCOME

Of the 55.3 million houses in the United States in 1956, some 12.6 million were substandard. Another 2 million were in neighborhoods so run-down that they were undesirable for children. Among the substandard dwellings were the 14.8 per cent of all houses (24.5 per cent in 1950) with no flush toilet, the 16.9 per cent with no bathtub or shower (26.8 per cent in 1950), and the 9.4 per cent with no inside water. Only 5 million of these were capable of being rehabilitated. Many of the irreparable ones were among the 6 million houses built before 1900 and still in use. The 1960 data reflect little improvement. Preliminary figures indicate that 5.2 per cent of all housing units were "dilapidated" and 14.4 per cent were "deteriorating." Exclusive of dilapidated housing, 13.6 per cent of all housing units lacked either hot water, a private toilet or bath, or running water. In all, 27 per cent of the nation's housing was below standard in 1960. In order to eliminate the substandard homes and prevent the growth of new slums, an average of 2.3 million housing units will have to be built annually between 1960 and 1975—far more than the present rate of construction of about 1.4 million housing units a year.[30]

About one-half of the income class earning less than $2,000 owned their homes in 1956 (compared to 80 per cent of the spending units of the richest income-fifth). But one-tenth of their homes were dilapidated, and another one-third lacked a basic facility like running water and flush toilets. For tenants with less than $2,000 income, the situation was even worse. Nearly one-quarter of their homes were dilapidated, and another one-third lacked a basic facility. More than one-quarter of the $2,000–$4,000 income class lived in such dilapidated or inadequate housing in 1956. In 1959, of the homeowners who earned less than $3,000, only 12 per cent had houses valued at $15,000 or more, compared to 60 per cent of those earning more than $7,500.[31]

The vast majority of the population is unable to purchase new homes. The median cost of a new, nonfarm dwelling was $13,700 in 1955. Assuming that housing costs should not consume more than a fifth (and in most cases they consume one-fourth or one-third) of a family's income, only one-tenth of the nation's families were able to buy and maintain such a house. Although many American families overextend themselves to purchase a new home, comparatively few of these earn less than $5,000.[32] For many families who have taken the credit risk of buying a new home since World War II, inflation has been the major factor preventing foreclosures.

From 1937 to 1953, when it lost momentum, the public housing program razed only 200,000 "slum" dwellings, a small fraction of the total. But slum clearance—which has been accompanied by a rather minor public housing program characterized by dull, unattractive apartment buildings —has often done more harm than good. The task of relocating displaced slum-dwellers has been primarily their own, and only a minority have moved back into the reconstructed neighborhood. In many instances—New York's East Side and Boston's West End are a few—they have been pushed into other slums to make room for the middle- and upper-income groups that will occupy the new, high-rental apartments built on the old site.

"It is now almost twenty years since the birth of the public housing program," Charles Abrams, a leading housing authority, observed in 1955. "If I were to sum up the most important political lessons I have learned since my association with it, they are that . . . once social reforms have won tonal appeal in the public mind, their slogans and goal-symbols may degenerate into tools of the dominant class for beleaguering the minority and often for defeating the very aims which the original sponsors had intended for their reforms."[33]

THE FOUNDATIONS OF INEQUALITY

The automobile is one of the most important economic status symbols, and alone accounts for one-half of all durable-goods expenditures by American consumers. Some 54 per cent of families and unattached individuals owned a car in 1935–36, 58 per cent in 1941, and 70 per cent in 1958. As soon as a family reaches the maintenance standard of living, it begins directing more of its income to automobiles and durable goods. Because half the population lives below the maintenance standard, the upper-income half accounts for a very large part of the high-status economic symbols—an inequality in distribution that is fundamentally a reflection of income inequalities.

Car ownership by income class is highly unequal. In 1959, 23 per cent of those earning less than $1,000 owned a car, compared to 95 per cent of those earning more than $10,000.[34]

Since anyone with $100 may own a car, the real issue in considering the distribution of automobiles as status symbols is the pattern of ownership of high-value cars. So let us turn our attention to new cars. In 1935–36, the top income-tenth purchased 40 per cent of the new cars. In 1952, the top 9 per cent, by income, of spending units purchased 33 per cent of the new cars; in 1953, the top 11 per cent purchased 36 per cent, and in 1954, 29 per cent.[35] A consistent pattern of more new-car purchases by the top-income group is clearly seen. The relationship between the value of the automobile owned and the owner's income class follows the income distribution pattern. In 1955, 29 per cent of those in the $7,500-and-over income class owned cars valued at $2,000 and up, compared to less than 1 per cent of those in the $0–$2,000 class. This distribution reflects the fact that in 1956, the poorer half of the spending units purchased a mere 12 per cent of the new cars.[36] Thus "massification"!

This pattern of inequality exists in all major durable-goods items—television sets, refrigerators, washing machines, furniture. It permeates every fiber of our lives, and influences the conditions of life and death, freedom and restraint, for all. In 1957, the richest 8 per cent, by income, enjoyed more days of vacation than the total enjoyed by the poorest third, by income. Less than half the homes of families and individuals in the $1,000–$1,500 bracket had telephones—contrasted to nearly all the homes in the $10,000-plus bracket.[37] This inequality of consumption could be illustrated by innumerable additional examples.

But what of the rich? We have been told that there is no longer a class consuming conspicuously, even if they do have the economic power to do so. They are, David Riesman suggests, "inconspicuous" consumers.

In late 1959, Tiffany & Company ("for the record only as the entire stock has been sold") advertised a fourteen-karat-gold putter for $1,475.[38] Shortly thereafter, Mr. and Mrs. Henry Ford II tossed a $100,000 coming-out party for their daughter. The trend toward splash began in the mid-1950's after years of comparative restraint. "The rich have been in hiding for twenty years," one fashionable interior decorator declared. "They are coming out of their holes. And they're having a ball."[39] *Fortune* magazine concluded that "rich Americans have begun to build big expensive houses again," those worth at least $250,000, and used 50 of them to illustrate its assertion, suggesting there were "many more."[40]

That here and there some wealthy gentleman has set himself up in a $750,000 house or yacht is altogether consistent with the facts of American life—the academic image of it notwithstanding. Although it has been possible for $30,000 Rolls-Royces, $3,500 silver coffeepots, and $18,000 Labrador minks to slip by unnoticed, it is clear that the 2.5 million butlers, maids, chauffeurs, and cooks employed in private households are paid by someone. And it is equally clear that the continuation of such extravagant consumption requires the extreme inequality of wealth that I have been describing throughout this book.

Some 28,000 Americans had a net worth of more than $500,000 in 1957—nearly twice as many as in 1945—according to the Dunhill International List Company, of New York. These are the people who, despite allegedly steep income and inheritance taxes, still manage to obtain the twenty-karat diamonds, the $300 suits, and the $2,500 gowns.[41]

The urban family or unattached individual in the $10,000-plus income class consumes eight times the dollar value of all goods consumed by the under-$1,000-income class, four times as much as the $2,000–$3,000 class, and twice as much as the $5,000–$6,000 class. These are not trivial distinctions; consumption varies as widely as income.

In conspicuous economic-status symbols, this inequality in consumption is even greater. The wealthier classes, especially those with an income exceeding $10,000, spend a great deal more on household operation, furnishings, and equipment.

Inequality, by income class, in all major areas of consumption, excluding savings, is illustrated in Appendix 2.* This table was calculated from data presented by the Bureau of Labor Statistics in its eighteen-volume *Study of Consumer Expenditures* for 1950, the most complete survey of its kind ever made. Fortunately, it includes credit purchases in its consumption data. However, it excludes rural families, both farm and nonfarm. Since income is distributed considerably

* Pp. 140–41.

more unevenly in rural areas than urban areas, the data in Appendix 2 understate somewhat the inequality in the national consumption by income classes. Nevertheless, the pattern of unequal consumption is clear. It is obvious that for individually consumed items, such as medical care and clothing, the significant fact is per-capita consumption, which takes into account family size. For jointly consumed items, such as housing and automobiles, the significant fact is the consumption of the family as a whole, and this accounts for the largest part of the total expenditures in every income class, especially the lower-income classes.[42] But for certain other items, the economies effected by purchasing them for an entire family substantially raise per-capita consumption above what would appear in purely per-capita calculations. In these areas, the index of inequality among income classes is presented on both a per-capita and spending-unit basis.

Even though the total consumption of goods of each income class may rise as its real income grows, the consumption gap between income classes will remain very great as long as income distribution remains inequitable. Equalized consumption of high economic-status symbols is impossible as long as wealth is concentrated in the few.

Differences in modes of living and consumption, dictated by differences in income, create a sharply stratified social order and a distinct class structure. Although absolute consumption may increase on every income level as real income gradually expands, the inequalities of income and consumption remain. This, at least, has been the pattern in the United States.

A rapidly developing technology requires an equally rapid increase in consumption. And it is the distribution of incomes among various classes, and not the absolute money income, that determines the ability of consumers to absorb the potential output and to maintain full employment in a potentially limitless industrial technology.

8

The Quality of Economic Life: Myth and Reality

Insofar as economic power in the United States derives from savings and income, it is dominated by a small class, comprising not more than one-tenth of the population, whose interests and style of life mark them off from the rest of American society. And within this class, a very small elite controls the corporate structure, the major sector of our economy, and through it makes basic price and investment decisions that directly affect the entire nation.

"The historic ethos of American life" may be "its bourgeois hungers, its classlessness, the spirit of equality," as Louis Hartz suggests in *The Liberal Tradition in America* (1955), but these are surely not the dominant realities in its social and economic structure.[1] American society is based on a class structure, and it pervades most of the crucial facets of life.

More than any other factor, the American class structure is determined by the great inequality in the distribution of income, an inequality that has not lessened although the economy's unemployment total has dropped from 12 million to a much smaller but still substantial figure. A sharp inequality of income has remained despite a generation of encroachments by laws, wars, and crises at home and abroad. If the form this inequality takes has been modified by expense accounts, undistributed profits, undeclared income, and similar complex measures, the nature of the phenomenon has not been altered.

The economically determined class lines in American society have been reinforced by the failure of the lowest-paid groups (largely blue-collar workers) to increase their relative income share since 1939—contrary to the common academic notion that they have. Their occasional ascents to a higher-income bracket usually result from the entry of wife or child into the labor market. And, perhaps most significant of all, the movement of the children of blue-collar workers into white-collar occupations is not necessarily a step upward, since white-collar workers are losing ground in their income standing.

Inequality of income is reflected in inequality of consumption, an inequality so great that contemporary social theories on the "democratization" or "massification" of symbols of economic status hold little relevance to the America of this decade. On the one hand, nearly one-half of the population is financially able to meet only its immediate physical needs, and the larger part of this group, nearly one-third of the nation, are in want of even basic necessities. On the other hand, a small section of the population, at most the top tenth, lives in the prosperous and frequently sumptuous manner that most social commentators ascribe to the large majority of Americans. And within this small section, there exists an economic elite variously described as the "sports-car," "country-club," or "Ivy League" set, depending on its particular tastes. Here are found the major owners of stock and the corporate managers, sharing the same social life and the same set of values.

Sharp inequalities in consumption are the pervasive fact of the American class structure. Privacy and comfort in housing are privileges of the well-to-do, and an increasing number of $250,000-and-up homes are being built throughout the United States—at a time when the few old mansions of the Astors and Morgans are being sold, purportedly because of loss of wealth, but actually because of changes in taste. The type of car one drives is a fairly accurate index of social class; the expensive sports car is purchased when an ordinary car will no longer impart sufficient prestige. Steaks are standard fare in the upper-income ranks; hamburger—which now accounts for one-quarter of beef consumption as opposed to one-tenth before World War II—is the staple of the luckier among the lower-income groups. Life is longer for the wealthy, whose money spares them from some diseases and in general gives them superior medical care. Last of all, higher education at the best institutions perpetuates the advantages of wealth in succeeding generations, while among the poor, vast reservoirs of talent and creativity go unexploited.

The basic economic fact of life for a majority of the population is insecurity. This is the logical outgrowth of their lack of ready savings; a very large majority of the low- and middle-income population have no more than a few months' income saved for financial emergencies.

Yet such emergencies are frequent among low-income families—in part because they are low-income families. The resultant increased rate of illness not only drains their meager finances, even with hospitalization insurance, but often has the disastrous effect of cutting off the earnings of the breadwinner.

Another common emergency for the low-income family is recurring unemployment, a by-product of the business cycle. If the family is covered by unemployment insurance—and over one-third of workers are not—the loss of income during this period is compensated for only very inadequately. If unemployment is very brief, the average family weathers it, although not without suffering reductions in consumption and other difficulties. If unemployment lasts more than several months, it eliminates the average family's savings, and causes a sharp reduction in consumption and perhaps some credit defaults. If unemployment compensation ends, relief is often the only recourse. For millions of Americans, this sequence of events is more than academic; they have experienced the necessity of having to live on $20 or $30 a week.

The insecurity caused by the ever-present possibility of unemployment, illness, or some other cause of financial emergency is made more ominous by the suddenness with which these crises occur. Perhaps more important is the expectation, growing out of personal experience and the observation of family and friends, that there is never enough money with which to meet predictable, certain responsibilities. Children add to the financial burdens of the average worker during the period when his income is greatest. By the time his financial responsibility for his children is ended, his peak earning period is past, and for himself and his wife, there is only the prospect of a continuation of the inadequate living standards of their late youth and early middle age. During the plateau between the children's attaining financial independence and the start of retirement, the average worker may save, but after retirement, he ends his life in want. If, before old age, he lived slightly below the maintenance level, he now drops below the emergency level.

For nearly half the population, these are the harsh facts of economic life—and for most, these facts limit their freedom to conceive or attain noneconomic goals.

It is true, as John Kenneth Galbraith suggests, that poverty is an "afterthought" in the contemporary American economy, but it is not true that the nation is so well off that we should "escape from the obsolete and contrived preoccupation associated with the assumption of poverty."[2] Poverty is an afterthought not because it *has* disappeared, but because social scientists *believe* it has.

In the coming decades, certain conditions giving rise to poverty will grow in importance, and if they meet the same response in future years as they have since World War II, the percentages of the population living at submaintenance and subemergency standards will climb, despite the increase in real income for some occupations. One such factor is the simultaneous numerical growth and relative economic decline of the white-collar class. This trend is a crucial aspect of a group that many social scientists thought would join that "classless" and nebulous category the middle class. Another element is the mounting number of families headed by women, a low-income group—in part because of wage prejudice. But, above all, there is the persistent growth in the population aged sixty-five and over, most of whom live on penurious Social Security payments or other meager funds.

It is conceivable that the termination of the business cycle, plus a substantial rise in real income, could end poverty in the United States caused by unemployment and low wages. But realization of these two goals is quite unlikely. Too many factors are operating to assure a continuing sequence of recessions, or even worse.

One difficulty in the way of full employment is the rising productivity per man-hour, and it is certain to become more formidable as automation spreads. The solution obviously is to expand consumption greatly, but only a decisive shift in the distribution of income and purchasing power can accomplish this. A self-defeating factor in wage boosts is the almost invariable business practice of passing along the cost of pay increases to the public. Raising legal minimum wages and extending the coverage to more people will not increase real purchasing power unless accompanied by direct control of prices.

Thus, eliminating poverty caused by unemployment and low wages requires the sweeping sort of political decisions concerning the economy which no administration has proposed or practiced, except during World War II. For this reason, it is probable that the very substantial importance of poverty caused by unemployment and low wages will not diminish in the near future. This static position, plus the rising new trends toward poverty discussed above, and the instability inherent in an extensive credit system—all these factors indicate that poverty will continue to be a basic aspect of the American social and class structure so long as no fundamental changes are made in the distribution of wealth and the autonomous control of the corporate machinery.

Poverty and low incomes in the United States are not, as in underdeveloped nations, an inevitable consequence of deficient industry. In 1958, only three-quarters of the nation's industrial capacity was utilized, and 5 million workers were unemployed. This was true in large part because the poorer half of the nation was not seriously in the market for new automobiles, refrigerators, houses, and goods of every other type. The problem was not in technology, but in economic organization, and at the bottom of this economic inadequacy was the sharply unequal distribution of income and wealth.

Let us ignore for the moment the tremendous industrial development that would be stimulated by the growth of the consumer-goods market among the poorer half of the population. Let us consider only that if the existing industrial machinery were fully exploited, its production would be sufficient to raise markedly the standard of living of those now living below the maintenance level.

Any valid social theory must be based on a reasonably correct empirical analysis. But it is impossible not to conclude that the social theories now dominant in the United States are dependent less on a valid analysis of American society than on illusion—the illusion that "economic equalitarianism" is a reality in the United States. But as my study has shown, the evidence refutes the basic assumption of universal abundance in America, which figures so centrally in current social thought.

Here lies the essential failure of contemporary theory: It does not fulfill the minimum function of social analysis, which is to attempt to describe the basic form and outline of society *as it is*. No one, in this age of intense methodological sophistication, expects a detailed description of reality in miniature, flawless and subject to no modification or revision. But social science does require a continuous, critical, uncomplaisant re-examination of premises and analyses, and in this respect, the dominant social theorists have failed.

There are, of course, some notable exceptions. David Riesman, for example, rejects the status quo's culture and values, although he accepts its economics. But he and the few other exceptions do not invalidate the proposition.

Instead of assuming such an attitude of criticism, contemporary social observers have become advocates of the equalitarian society they believe to exist. Conservative in their approach, they neither draw implications for the future nor point to any shortcomings in the present. Instead, they hail the accomplishments of the status quo. In this way, they avoid the need to subject their assertions to any rigorous scrutiny. For if the existing social order is achieving success in providing equality of opportunity, developing human resources, and eliminating economic instability, then no changes are needed.

It was not my purpose to recommend any partial laws or reforms with which to meet the far-reaching problems I have described. Rather, I have attempted to focus attention on the economic realities of our society, and on the disparity between them and the dominant theories on equality and economic justice in the United States.

Perhaps the ideal of a social and economic democracy—the type of society erroneously said to exist in the United States today—will at least serve as the stimulus for its ultimate creation.

Appendixes

INCOME-TENTH RANK OF MALE, EXPERIENCED CIVILIAN WAGE
OR SALARY WORKERS IN SELECTED OCCUPATIONS, ON BASIS OF
AVERAGE WAGE OR SALARY INCOME IN 1949

NOTES TO APPENDIX 1

The percentage of all occupational classes, excluding farmers, farm labor, and nonreporters, covered by the data in Appendix 1 is 67.3.

n.e.c. = not elsewhere classified.

(1) indicates the highest tenth, (2) the second highest, (10) the lowest tenth, etc. A plus sign (+) indicates the highest third of that tenth, a minus sign (—) the lowest third. The Survey Research Center's data on the highest and lowest income received by each tenth includes income from property in determining the ranges. Since this form of income is relatively minor in the lower and middle income-tenths, the major error is to be found in the underestimation of the lowest income range of the richest tenths. Since only a very small percentage of lower- and middle-income earners receive property income, its exclusion here is not important. The rich rank in the upper tenths on the basis of their wage and salary income alone.

Source: All data on average incomes are taken from Census tables published in Herman P. Miller, *Income of the American People* (New York: John Wiley & Sons, 1955), pp. 173–76. Income-tenth ranges are from the *Federal Reserve Bulletin*, July, 1954, p. 700. Total male occupational data are from the Bureau of the Census, *Statistical Abstract of the United States—1952* (Washington, D.C.: Government Printing Office, 1952), p. 186.

	Income-Tenth Rank
Professional, Technical, and Kindred Workers	
Artists and art teachers	3+
Authors, editors, reporters	2+
Chemists	2—

Income-Tenth
Rank

Professional, Technical, and Kindred Workers (continued)

Clergymen	6
College presidents, professors, instructors (n.e.c.)	2—
Designers and draftsmen	4+
Engineers—civil	2
Engineers—electrical	2
Engineers—mechanical	2+
Musicians and music teachers	4
Pharmacists	3—
Social, welfare, and recreation workers	4—
Sports instructors, athletes, and entertainers	4—
Teachers (n.e.c.)	4

Percentage of total occupational class covered: 42.5.

Salaried Managers and Officials

Railroad conductors	3+
Postmasters and miscellaneous government officials	3
Managers and officials	
Manufacturing	1
Transportation, communications, public utilities	2+
Wholesale trade	1
Eating and drinking places	4—
Retail trade, except eating and drinking	2—
Finance, insurance, and real estate	1
Business and repair services	2+
Personal services	3—

Percentage of total occupational class covered: 31.7.

Clerical, Sales, and Kindred Workers

Baggagemen, express messengers, and railroad mail clerks	4
Bookkeepers, accountants, cashiers, ticket agents	4+
Mail carriers	5+
Messengers—except express	8—
Shipping and receiving clerks	6+
Stenographers, typists, and secretaries	3—
Telegraph operators	4—
Newsboys	10
Insurance agents and brokers	3
Real estate agents and brokers	3
Salesmen and sales clerks (n.e.c.)	4—

Percentage of total occupational class covered: 59.6.

Income-Tenth
Rank

Craftsmen, Foremen, and Kindred Workers

Bakers	5—
Blacksmiths, forgemen, and hammermen	5—
Boilermakers	4—
Cabinetmakers and patternmakers	5
Carpenters	6—
Compositors and typesetters	4+
Electricians	4
Foremen (n.e.c.)	
Construction	4+
Manufacturing	3+
Transportation, communication, and other	
public utilities	3—
Inspectors (n.e.c.)	4
Linemen and servicemen—telegraph, etc.	4—
Locomotive engineers	2—
Locomotive firemen	4+
Machinists, millwrights, and toolmakers	4—
Masons, tile setters, and stonecutters	5
Mechanics, repairmen, and loom fixers	5—
Metal molders	5—
Painters (construction), and paperhangers	6
Plasterers and cement finishers	5
Plumbers and pipe fitters	4
Printing craftsmen—except compositors and typesetters	3+
Rollers and roll hands	4—
Roofers and sheet-metal workers	5
Shoemakers and repairers—except factory	7
Stationary engineers, cranemen, and hoistmen	4
Structural-metal workers	4
Tailors and furriers	5

Percentage of total occupational class covered: 83.4.

Operatives and Kindred Workers

Apprentices	7+
Auto-service and parking attendants	7—
Railroad brakemen and switchmen	4
Deliverymen and drivers—bus, taxi, and truck	6+
Stationary firemen	5—
Mine operatives and laborers (n.e.c.)	6
Motormen—railroad, mine, factory, etc.	5+
Painters—except construction and maintenance	6+
Sailors and deck hands	6
Welders and flame-cutters	5+

	Income-Tenth Rank

Operatives and Kindred Workers (n.e.c.)

Food and kindred industries	6
Knitting mills	5—
Textile mills—except knitting mills	7+
Apparel and other fabric-textile production	5—
Furniture, and lumber and wood	7—
Paper industries and printing	6+
Chemicals, petroleum, and coal	5+
Rubber	5
Footwear industries—except rubber	7+
Leather production—except footwear	6—
Stone, clay, and glass	6+
Iron and steel, except specialty metal industries	5—
Nonferrous metals	6+
Machinery	5—
Motor vehicles and equipment	5
Transportation equipment—except motor vehicles	5

Percentage of total occupational class covered: 76.3.

Service Workers

Private household workers	8—
Firemen	4—
Guards and watchmen	6
Policemen, sheriffs, and marshals	5+
Barbers, beauticians, and manicurists	7+
Charmen, janitors, and porters	7—
Cooks—except private household	6—
Elevator operators	7
Waiters, bartenders, and counter workers	7
Service workers, except private household (n.e.c.)	8—

Percentage of total occupational class covered: 84.0.

Laborers—Except Farmers and Miners

Fishermen and oystermen	6—
Longshoremen and stevedores	6
Lumbermen, raftsmen, and woodchoppers	8
Laborers (n.e.c.)	
Manufacturing industries	
Food and kindred products	7+
Textiles, textile products, and apparel	7—
Furniture and lumber and wood products	8
Paper, paper products, and printing	6—

	Income-Tenth Rank
Chemicals, petroleum, and coal products	6
Stone, clay, and glass products	7+
Iron and steel—except specialty metal industries	6—
Nonferrous metals and products	6—
Machinery	6—
Motor vehicles and equipment	6	
Transportation equipment—except motor vehicles	7+
Nonmanufacturing industries	
Construction	7—
Railroads and railroad express	7+
Transportation—except railroad	7+
Telecommunications, utilities, and sanitary services	7+
Wholesale and retail trade	8+

Percentage of total occupational class covered: 79.1.

	Per-centage of Urban Spending Units	Average Family Size	Total Expenditures for Current Consumption (In dollars)	Index of Total Expenditures		Food and Beverages		Tobacco	Housing	Fuel, Light, and Refrigeration
				S.U.	P.C.	S.U.	P.C.	P.C.	S.U.	S.U.
Income Class			(100 = Expenditure of Under-$1,000 Income Class)							
Under $1,000	6.3	1.5	1278	100	100	100	100	100	100	100
$1,000–$2,000	12.3	2.1	1768	138	99	145	104	171	116	111
$2,000–$3,000	18.7	2.7	2718	213	118	213	118	215	146	136
$3,000–$4,000	24.0	3.2	3570	279	131	265	124	219	172	161
$4,000–$5,000	16.9	3.4	4450	348	154	313	138	247	203	183
$5,000–$6,000	9.5	3.6	5257	411	171	359	150	242	225	202
$6,000–$7,500	6.4	3.7	6043	473	192	397	161	257	259	218
$7,500–$10,000	3.5	4.0	7108	557	209	465	174	258	295	250
$10,000-and-over	2.4	3.7	10773	843	342	598	242	300	482	315
Age of Spending-Unit Head			(100 = Expenditure of Spending-Unit Heads Under 25 Years of Age)							
Under 25 years	3.8	2.5	3142	100	100	100	100	100	100	100
25–35 years	21.8	3.3	3870	123	93	130	99	90	115	187
35–45 years	23.1	3.6	4360	139	96	152	105	85	121	245
45–55 years	20.4	3.1	4342	137	111	149	120	97	118	248
55–65 years	16.4	2.6	3657	116	112	129	124	92	104	241
65–75 years	10.4	2.1	2567	82	97	93	111	69	86	213
75 years-and-over	4.1	1.9	2076	66	87	76	101	52	79	221

NOTES TO APPENDIX 2

Index figures are given either in spending-unit (S.U.) or per-capita (P.C.) terms, using the more applicable category. In the case of per-capita expenditures, the average dollar expenditure per item of each income or age class was divided by the average spending-unit size in that class and then indexed on the basis of the lowest income class or youngest age group in order to show absolute

Household Operation	Furnishings and Equipment	Clothing and Clothing Services	Automobile	Other Transportation	Medical Care	Personal Care	Recreation	Reading	Education	Miscellaneous	
S.U.	S.U.	P.C.	S.U.	P.C.	P.C.	P.C.	P.C.	S.U.	P.C.	S.U.	P.C.
(100 = Expenditure of Under-$1,000 Income Class)											
100	100	100	100	100	100	100	100	100	100	100	100
130	158	146	137	154	75	123	119	129	70	80	57
179	316	194	330	161	88	146	195	193	137	111	62
230	431	226	571	143	101	155	278	243	174	111	52
295	598	281	778	165	110	174	365	286	274	149	66
375	689	336	992	199	116	193	403	321	348	217	91
444	787	392	1149	221	134	207	494	379	489	249	101
614	825	452	1315	272	154	222	522	421	641	271	102
1532	1649	770	1619	417	199	325	931	600	1622	886	360
(100 = Expenditure of Spending-Unit Heads Under 25 Years of Age)											
100	100	100	100	100	100	100	100	100	100	100	100
162	111	89	111	72	95	95	95	130	51	157	119
198	115	101	104	83	101	100	95	141	99	257	179
193	97	118	105	122	126	116	108	141	186	410	330
169	76	104	88	142	142	116	89	130	112	319	307
126	49	74	54	117	149	91	64	96	30	210	250
156	29	58	34	84	133	72	40	93	21 ·	148	194

consumption inequalities. Items tabulated on a spending-unit basis were not divided by size of unit.

Source: Calculated from data given in Bureau of Labor Statistics and Wharton School of Finance and Commerce, *Study of Consumer Expenditures, Incomes and Savings* (Philadelphia: University of Pennsylvania Press, 1957), XVIII, 2, 3, 10, 11.

Notes

Introduction

1. Frederick Lewis Allen, *The Big Change* (New York: Harper & Brothers, 1952), p. ix.
2. Joseph J. Spengler, "Changes in Income Distribution and Social Stratification: A Note," *American Journal of Sociology,* November, 1953, p. 253.
3. David Riesman *et al., The Lonely Crowd* (Garden City, N.Y.: Doubleday & Company, 1953), pp. 95 ff.
4. David E. Lilienthal, *Big Business: A New Era* (New York: Harper & Brothers, 1953), p. 202.
5. Shepard B. Clough, *The American Way: The Economic Basis of Our Civilization* (New York: Thomas Y. Crowell Company, 1953), p. 167. See also Eric F. Goldman, *Rendezvous with Destiny* (New York: Alfred A. Knopf, 1952), pp. 436 ff.; Thomas C. Cochran, *The American Business System: A Historical Perspective, 1900–1950* (Cambridge, Mass.: Harvard University Press, 1957), pp. 110, 156–57, 186–87; William Petersen, "Is America Still the Land of Opportunity?" *Commentary,* November, 1953, pp. 477–86.

Chapter 1: Trends in the Distribution of Income

1. Will Lissner, in the *New York Times,* March 5, 1952, p. 1.
2. Tax Foundation, *Fiscal Facts for '58* (New York: Tax Foundation, 1958), p. 9; Selma F. Goldsmith, "Income Distribution by Size—1955–58," *Survey of Current Business,* April, 1959, p. 10.
3. Henry C. Wallich, in *People's Capitalism,* ed. David M. Potter (New York: The Advertising Council, 1957), p. 11.
4. Selma F. Goldsmith, "Appraisal of Basic Data Available for Constructing Income Size Distributions," *Studies in Income and Wealth* (New York: National Bureau of Economic Research, 1951), XIII, 284, 302; Selma F. Goldsmith, "The Relation of Census Income Distribution Statistics to Other Income Data," *Studies in Income and Wealth* (New York: National Bureau of Economic Research, 1958), XXIII, 70–75.

5. In the post-1941 period, working wives added considerably to the incomes of a large percentage of the families, and it is clear that the spending-unit calculations are the most satisfactory. In 1918–19, however, wives and children earned only 10 per cent of the total family income, and, since a number of these wives were also heads of households, it is apparent that the "recipient" definition introduces no great bias into the figures. This is especially true of our understanding of the income share of the richest tenth. In 1919, among the richest 1 per cent of the population, income-tax returns submitted by wives represented only 3.2 per cent of the total, and 5.3 per cent in 1934–36. Only 15 per cent of individual wage earners in 1935–36 were female supplementary earners. See Temporary National Economic Committee (hereafter cited as TNEC), *Concentration and Composition of Individual Incomes, 1918–1937* (Washington, D.C.: Government Printing Office, 1940), Monograph No. 4, p. 81; W. S. Woytinsky, *Earnings and Social Security in the United States* (Washington, D.C.: Social Science Research Council, 1943), pp. 50–51.

6. Definitions are taken from U.S. Senate, Committee on Banking and Currency, *Income and Housing,* Staff Report, 85th Cong., 1st Sess. (Washington, D.C.: Government Printing Office, 1957), pp. 64–72; *Federal Reserve Bulletin* (hereafter cited as *FRB*), July, 1959, p. 701; Bureau of the Census, *Current Population Reports,* P-60, No. 27, pp. 16–17. The Office of Business Economics data on size distributions show a substantially smaller percentage of the population in lower-income classes than do Census data, and somewhat more in the upper classes. Survey Research Center data, which are much closer to agreement with the OBE than with Census data, are utilized whenever possible, since they are far more extensive than the OBE data. Where no alternate data are available, Census data are utilized. See Goldsmith, "The Relation of Census Income Distribution . . . ," *op. cit.,* pp. 83–91.

7. National Industrial Conference Board (hereafter cited as NICB), *Studies in Enterprise and Social Progress* (New York: National Industrial Conference Board, 1939), p. 123; Don D. Lescohier, *Working Conditions* in *History of Labor in the United States,* ed. John R. Commons (New York: The Macmillan Company, 1935), III, 55. Independent data verifying the NICB data can be found, for 1918, in Wesley C. Mitchell *et al., Income in the United States, 1910–1918* (New York: National Bureau of Economic Research, 1921), I, 134–35; for 1929, in Maurice Leven *et al., America's Capacity to Consume* (Washington, D.C.: Brookings Institution, 1934), p. 96; for 1935–36, National Resources Committee, *Consumer Incomes in the United States* (Washington, D.C.: Government Printing Office, 1938), p. 95.

8. Detailed data on this trend can be found in Selma Goldsmith *et al.,* "Size Distribution of Income Since the Mid-Thirties," *Review of Economics and Statistics,* February, 1954, pp. 1–32; Jesse Burkhead,

"Living Standards and Productivity," *Review of Economics and Statistics,* August, 1951, p. 247; *Monthly Labor Review,* September, 1942, p. 421.

9. Bureau of Labor Statistics, *Family Spending and Saving in Wartime* (Washington, D.C.: Government Printing Office, 1945), Bulletin No. 822, p. 94; and Nathan M. Koffsky and Jeanne E. Lear, "Size Distribution of Farm Operators' Income in 1946," *Studies in Income and Wealth* (New York: National Bureau of Economic Research, 1951), XIII, 243. In 1935–36 the distribution of income-in-kind among the nation's families was about equal for food; but for housing it was very much greater among the rich. See National Resources Committee, *Consumer Expenditures in the United States* (Washington, D.C.: Government Printing Office, 1939), p. 79.

10. Department of Agriculture, *1957 Agricultural Outlook Charts* (Washington, D.C.: Government Printing Office, 1956), p. 30.

11. *Wall Street Journal,* March 18, 1958, p. 1; also p. 1 on the following dates: October 29, November 11 and 13, 1957; February 14 and 21, March 13 and 18, 1958.

12. William H. Whyte, Jr., "The Cadillac Phenomenon," *Fortune,* February, 1955, pp. 106–11; "Expense Accounts: A $5 Billion Tax Deduction, and Growing," *U.S. News & World Report,* August 16, 1957, pp. 83–88; Ernest Havemann, "The Expense Account Aristocracy," *Life,* March 9, 1953, pp. 140–42; Harvey S. Berman, "He's on an Expense Account," *Challenge,* March, 1956, pp. 55–58. For credit cards, see Robert Bendiner, "Credit Cards: The Thirty-Day Tycoons," *The Reporter,* February 5, 1959, pp. 26–30.

13. "Expense Accounts," *Harvard Business Review,* March–April, 1960, pp. 16, 172; Randolph Paul, *Taxation in the United States* (Boston: Little, Brown & Co., 1954), p. 618; *U.S. News & World Report,* August 16, 1957, p. 87; also "Expense Account Scandal," *ibid.,* January 25, 1960, pp. 50–56.

14. *Ibid.,* August 16, 1957, p. 83; and V. Henry Rothschild and Rudolf Sobernheim, "Expense Accounts for Executives," *Yale Law Journal,* July, 1958.

15. See C. Harry Kahn, "Entrepreneurial Income," *38th Annual Report, National Bureau of Economic Research, 1958,* pp. 84–85. On the other hand, Frederick D. Stocker and John C. Ellickson, "How Fully Do Farmers Report Their Incomes?" *National Tax Journal,* June, 1959, pp. 116–26, claim that tax evasion by farmers in 1952 was only 18 per cent of their income, 16 per cent in 1953, and 13 per cent in 1955—or no larger than for most occupational classes. Data given in C. Harry Kahn, "Coverage of Entrepreneurial Income on Federal Tax Returns," in U.S. House of Representatives, Committee on Ways and Means, *Tax Revision Compendium,* 86th Cong., 1st Sess. (Washington, D.C.: Government Printing Office, 1959), II, 1449, show that 56 per cent

of the undeclared entrepreneurial income in 1957 was accounted for by the business and professional classes.

16. Robert Wasson, Abner Hurwitz, and Irving Schweiger, "Field Surveys of Consumer Income—An Appraisal," *Studies in Income and Wealth*, XIII, 518.

17. National Bureau of Economic Research, *The National Economic Accounts of the United States* (Washington, D.C.: Government Printing Office, 1958), p. 110.

18. Daniel M. Holland and C. Harry Kahn, "Comparison of Personal and Taxable Income," in U.S. Senate, Joint Committee on the Economic Report, *Federal Tax Policy for Economic Growth and Stability*, 84th Cong., 1st Sess. (Washington, D.C.: Government Printing Office, 1955), p. 320; Goldsmith, "Appraisal of Basic Data . . . ," *op. cit.*, p. 302; Daniel M. Holland, "Unreporting of Dividends and Interest on Tax Returns," *Tax Revision Compendium*, II, 1399, 1403, 1418; Kahn, "Coverage of Entrepreneurial Income on Federal Tax Returns," *ibid.*, II, 1439–61.

19. George Katona *et al.*, "Stock Ownership Among American Families," *Michigan Business Review*, January, 1953, p. 14.

20. Calculated from data in Bureau of Internal Revenue, *The Audit Control Program: A Summary of Preliminary Results* (Washington, D.C.: Government Printing Office, 1951), p. 20. Holland, "Unreporting of Dividends and Interest . . . ," *op. cit.*, p. 1415, claims that the $7,000-plus returns accounted for 66 per cent of the missing dividends and 38 per cent of the interest.

21. Bureau of Internal Revenue, *op. cit.*, p. 21. Lower-income returns generally report most of their interest receipts. See Lawrence H. Seltzer, *Interest as a Source of Personal Income and Tax Revenue* (New York: National Bureau of Economic Research, 1955), Occasional Paper 51, pp. 1257–58.

22. William Crum *et al.*, *Fiscal Planning for Total War* (New York: National Bureau of Economic Research, 1942), p. 278.

23. Lawrence H. Seltzer, *The Nature and Tax Treatment of Capital Gains and Losses* (New York: National Bureau of Economic Research, 1951), p. 221; data for 1946–59 from *Economic Report of the President —1960*, p. 220.

24. *Montgomery's Federal Taxes* (35th ed.; New York: The Ronald Press Company, 1954), Part 5, p. 37. For corporate tax evasion, see Raymond W. Goldsmith, *A Study of Saving in the United States* (Princeton, N.J.: Princeton University Press, 1955). I, 969, II, 549–50; and William F. Hellmuth, Jr., "The Corporate Income Tax Base," *Tax Revision Compendium*, I, 283–316.

25. Ralph Ross and Ernest van den Haag, *The Fabric of Society: An Introduction to the Social Sciences* (New York: Harcourt, Brace & Company, 1957), p. 387; Clough, *op. cit.*, p. 189; National Bureau of

Economic Research press release, May 21, 1951, p. 2; Simon Kuznets, *Shares of Upper Income Groups in Income and Savings* (New York: National Bureau of Economic Research, 1953).

26. All data from Kuznets, *op. cit.*, pp. 635, 637; and Bureau of the Census, *Statistical Abstract of the United States—1952* (Washington, D.C.: Government Printing Office, 1952), p. 261.

27. Kuznets, *op. cit.*, p. 54.

28. *Ibid.*, pp. 40 ff.

29. Bureau of the Census, *Statistical Abstract of the United States—1957* (Washington, D.C.: Government Printing Office, 1957), p. 315; Shirley S. Hoffman, "Agriculture as a Buyer," *Business Record,* June, 1959, p. 279; *Economic Report of the President—1960,* p. 229.

30. Kuznets, *op. cit.*, pp. xxxiii, 109–10.

31. *Ibid.*, p. 157.

32. For a discussion of this problem, see Selma F. Goldsmith "Size Distribution of Income . . . ," *op. cit.*, p. 18.

33. Office of Business Economics, *Income Distribution in the United States, 1944–1950* (Washington, D.C.: Government Printing Office, 1953), p. 15; *Survey of Current Business,* March, 1955, p. 24; *ibid.*, May, 1961, p. 19; Bureau of the Census, *Statistical Abstract of the United States—1959* (Washington, D.C.: Government Printing Office, 1959), p. 316.

34. Kuznets, *op. cit.*, pp. 447 ff., 459.

35. Daniel Creamer, *Personal Income During Business Cycles* (Princeton, N.J.: Princeton University Press, 1956), chap. vii.

36. Kuznets, *op. cit.*, pp. 36–38.

37. Computed from data given in *Economic Report of the President—1958,* p. 179; and Kuznets, *op. cit.*, p. 257. Allan M. Cartter, "Income Shares of the Upper Income Groups in Great Britain and the United States," *American Economic Review,* December, 1954, pp. 875–83, makes the point that if all undistributed profits were added to the shares of the upper 5 per cent, this group would have received 25.0 per cent of all income in 1937 and 23.7 per cent in 1948.

Chapter 2: *Taxation and Inequality*

1. Ross and Van den Haag, *op. cit.*, p. 398.

2. Roy G. and Gladys C. Blakey, *The Federal Income Tax* (New York: Longmans, Green & Co., 1940), pp. 366–73; and Louis Eisenstein, "The Rise and Decline of the Estate Tax," *Federal Tax Policy for Economic Growth,* pp. 830 ff.

3. Office of Business Economics, *National Income, 1954* (Washington, D.C.: Government Printing Office, 1954), p. 171.

4. All calculations from data in Bureau of Internal Revenue, *Statistics of Income for 1939, Part I* (Washington, D.C.: Government Print-

ing Office, 1942), pp. 63–64, and *Statistics of Income—Individual Income Tax Returns for 1957* (Washington, D.C.: Government Printing Office, 1959), p. 20.

5. J. Keith Butters *et al.*, *Effects of Taxation—Investment by Individuals* (Boston: Harvard Business School, 1953), p. 85.

6. Creamer, *op. cit.*, p. 153; Bureau of Internal Revenue, *Statistics of Income—Individual Returns for 1957*, p. 23.

7. Joseph A. Pechman, "What Would a Comprehensive Individual Income Tax Yield?" *Tax Revision Compendium*, I, 258.

8. Crum, *op. cit.*, pp. 172, 174; *Economic Report of the President—1958*, p. 174; Tax Foundation, *Reexamining the Federal Corporation Income Tax* (New York: Tax Foundation, 1958), p. 22; *The Budget of the United States Government for the Fiscal Year Ending June 30, 1960* (Washington, D.C.: Government Printing Office, 1959), p. M-12.

9. Selma F. Goldsmith, "Income Distribution by Size—1955–58," *op. cit.*, p. 16.

10. C. Harry Kahn, "Personal Expense Deductions," *37th Annual Report, National Bureau of Economic Research, 1957*, p. 49.

11. Holland and Kahn, *op. cit.*, pp. 331–32.

12. Bureau of Internal Revenue, *Statistics of Income—1957*, p. 37; Lawrence H. Seltzer, "The Individual Income Tax," *39th Annual Report, National Bureau of Economic Research, 1959*, p. 74.

13. Holland and Kahn, *op. cit.*, p. 333.

14. Tax Foundation, *Federal Excise Taxes* (New York: Tax Foundation, 1956), p. 47.

15. *Wall Street Journal*, May 5, 1958, p. 1.

16. Lewis H. Kimmel, *Taxes and Economic Incentives* (Washington, D.C.: Brookings Institution, 1950), p. 182.

17. Even this inadequate progression is an improvement over the distribution of the total Federal, state, and local tax burden in 1938–39. In that fiscal year, the total Federal tax burden as a percentage of the income of every income class was about equal in every income class up to $10,000 (roughly equal to $20,000 in 1958), when it began to rise steeply. State and local taxes, as a whole, were mildly regressive. See TNEC, *Who Pays the Taxes?* (Washington, D.C.: Government Printing Office, 1940), Monograph No. 3, p. 6.

18. Allen, *op. cit.*, p. 286.

19. Tax Foundation, *Allocation of the Tax Burden by Income Class*, pp. 14–15; Bureau of the Census, *Statistical Abstract—1959*, p. 368.

20. All quotations from *Wall Street Journal*, April 9, 1959, p. 1.

21. Bureau of Internal Revenue, *Statistics of Income—1957*, pp. 24–25.

22. Quoted in Arch Patton, "Executive Compensation: Tax Gimmicks vs. Incentives," *Harvard Business Review*, November–December,

1953, p. 114. For a general survey of executive tax avoidance, see Robert Schulman, "Tax Differentials in Executive Compensation," *Income Tax Differentials* (Princeton, N.J.: Tax Institute, 1958), pp. 67–81.

23. Seltzer, *The Nature and Tax Treatment of Capital Gains and Losses*, pp. 242 ff.

24. *Proxy Statement, General Motors Corporation, 1958*, p. 13.

25. NICB, *Compensation of Top Executives*, "Studies in Personnel Policy," No. 173 (New York. National Industrial Conference Board, 1959), p. 12; *U.S. News & World Report*, March 18, 1955, p. 27; May 11, 1959, pp. 84–85; U.S. Senate Committee on the Judiciary, *Study in Administered Prices in the Steel Industry*, Report of the Committee, 85th Cong., 2nd Sess. (Washington, D.C.: Government Printing Office, 1958), pp. 110–11. Data on General Dynamics, Douglas, and Pittsburgh from their 1957 proxy statements.

26. Raymond W. Goldsmith, *op. cit.*, III, 374, estimates that in 1944 the estates valued at $100,000 and over owned as much as 98 per cent of the wholly tax-exempt Federal, state, and local bonds. An excellent survey of tax avoidance laws is Stanley S. Surrey, "The Income Tax Base for Individuals," *Income Tax Differentials* (Princeton, N.J.: Tax Institute, 1958), pp. 34–58.

27. Eisenstein, *op. cit.*, pp. 833–36.

28. René A. Wormser, "How to Save Money by Giving It Away," *U.S. News & World Report*, December 28, 1956, p. 111.

29. Eisenstein, *op. cit.*, pp. 837 ff.

30. Stanley S. Surrey, "The Congress and the Tax Lobbyist—How Special Tax Provisions Get Enacted," *Harvard Law Review*, May, 1957, p. 1150; see also the pessimistic conclusions of Randolph Paul, *op. cit.*, pp. 763 ff., on the failure of progressive taxation.

Chapter 3: The Distribution of Wealth

1. *FRB*, September, 1953, pp. 11–12 of the reprint including extra data not appearing in the regular article. The Survey Research Center study is, by admission of its authors, conservative in its estimate of the net worth of the top-income class. This is due to sampling limitations and to the exclusion from the study of insurance, trust funds, corporate bonds, state, local, and foreign bonds, annuities, pension reserves, and a considerable portion of all liquid assets. (*Ibid.*, pp. 7–8; Raymond W. Goldsmith, *op. cit.*, III, 103.) Thus, the study overlooks a sizable share of the actual total assets that is heavily concentrated in the economic elite. The SRC estimate for 1953 repeated most of its errors for 1949, when it had calculated the distribution of assets on the basis of an estimated total of $613 billion. Raymond Goldsmith, the leading sav-

ings economist, more accurately fixed the total as $952 billion (*Op. cit.,* III, 107.)

In a more detailed chart on the distribution of total assets and net worth in early 1950, Goldsmith shows that the top-income 5 per cent of the spending units—those earning $7,500-plus in 1949—owned 33 per cent of the net worth. (*Ibid.,* p. 126.) The top income class of 1953, however, included 9 per cent of the spending units as opposed to 5 per cent for 1950. Assuming that in 1953 the wealthiest 5 per cent of spending units owned 33 per cent of the net worth, as they did in 1950, and, conservatively, that the lower 5 per cent of spending units in the top income-tenth were only half as wealthy, the richest 9 per cent (on a pro-rata basis) owned over 46 per cent of the net worth. There is probably a margin of error in this adjusted figure, but it is very likely much smaller than that in the SRC data.

In a somewhat parallel study, using Federal estate-tax returns, Robert J. Lampman estimated that in 1953 about 1 per cent of the population owned 24 per cent of all assets of the household sector of the economy, including two-thirds of the corporate stock and four-fifths of the state and local bonds. See "The Distribution of Wealth According to Estate Tax Returns," *39th Annual Report, National Bureau of Economic Research, 1959,* pp. 40–41. Lampman's data is further developed in "Changes in the Share of Wealth Held by Top Wealth-Holders, 1922–1956," *Review of Economics and Statistics,* November, 1959, pp. 379–92. Basing his findings on estate-tax returns, Lampman ignores the problem of inaccurate reporting, the extent to which many members of the economic elite now make their property arrangements before death to avoid estate taxes, and the inaccuracies in the 1953 Survey Research Center data on wealth distribution against which he compares his results. For the liabilities of using estate-tax returns, see William L. Crum, *The Distribution of Wealth* (Boston: Harvard Business School, 1935), Research Studies No. 13.

2. *FRB,* September, 1951, p. 1063. James S. Duesenberry, *Income, Saving and the Theory of Consumer Behavior* (Cambridge, Mass.: Harvard University Press, 1949), develops this fact in a criticism of Keynes's theory of savings-investment regulation.

3. Butters, *op. cit.,* p. 28, also makes this assertion.

4. Survey Research Center, *1960 Survey of Consumer Finances* (Ann Arbor, Mich.: Survey Research Center, 1961), p. 77.

5. *Ibid.,* p. 80.

6. *Ibid.*

7. *FRB,* June, 1956, p. 572.

8. Raymond W. Goldsmith, "Trends and Structural Changes in Savings in the Twentieth Century," *Savings in the Modern Economy,* ed. Walter W. Heller *et al.* (Minneapolis, Minn.: University of Minnesota Press, 1953), p. 151.

9. Ross and Van den Haag, *op. cit.,* p. 393.

10. Adolf A. Berle, Jr., *Power Without Property* (New York: Harcourt, Brace & Company, 1959), chaps. i–iii; Peter F. Drucker, *America's Next Twenty Years* (New York: Harper & Brothers, 1957), chap. iii.

11. TNEC, *The Distribution of Ownership in the 200 Largest Nonfinancial Corporations* (Washington, D.C.: Government Printing Office, 1940), Monograph No. 29, p. 18.

12. TNEC, *Survey of Shareholdings in 1,710 Corporations with Securities Listed on a National Securities Exchange* (Washington, D.C.: Government Printing Office, 1941), Monograph No. 30, p. 241.

13. Lewis H. Kimmel, *Share Ownership in the United States* (Washington, D.C.: Brookings Institution, 1952), pp. 43, 46.

14. Butters, *op. cit.,* p. 382.

15. TNEC, Monograph 29, p. 9; Kimmel, *Share Ownership in the United States,* p. 68.

16. Survey Research Center, *Stock Ownership Among American Families* (Ann Arbor, Mich.: Survey Research Center, June, 1960); Kimmel, *Share Ownership in the United States,* p. 95; Butters, *op. cit.,* p. 25; Katona, *op. cit.,* pp. 14 ff.

17. See, for example, A. H. Raskin, " 'Town Meeting' of the Shareholders," *New York Times Magazine,* May 12, 1957, p. 15; *Wall Street Journal,* April 26, 1960, p. 4. The Stock Exchange's data were collected by a market-research agency, and were utilized as part of the advertising campaign on "people's capitalism." Given the close agreement between the SRC and Brookings studies, and the questionable reliability of the Stock Exchange data, there is no need to debate the differences between the two sets of findings. A technical criticism appears in the SRC's June, 1960, study.

18. *Wall Street Journal,* September 10, 1959, p. 1; other articles of interest in the *Wall Street Journal* appear in the issues of April 8, May 26, August 25, October 7, 1959; March 8, 1960.

19. Adolf A. Berle, Jr., "Marx Was Wrong and So Is Khrushchev," *New York Times Magazine,* November 1, 1959, p. 95; also *Power Without Property.*

20. *Wall Street Journal,* April 11, 1960, p. 2.

21. Robert Tilove, *Pension Funds and Economic Freedom* (New York: Fund for the Republic, 1959); Paul P. Harbrecht, *Pension Funds and Economic Power* (New York: Twentieth Century Fund, 1959), pp. 115–18, 244.

Chapter 4: The Concentration of Corporate Power

1. Riesman, *op. cit.,* p. 252.

2. Adolf A. Berle, Jr., *The 20th Century Capitalist Revolution* (New York: Harcourt, Brace & Company, 1954), p. 182.

3. *Ibid.,* p. 60.

4. Lilienthal, *op. cit.,* p. 28.

5. Data for 1937 are calculated from TNEC Monograph No. 29, pp. 23, 350–54; data for 1955 are calculated from "The *Fortune* Directory of the 500 Largest U.S. Industrial Corporations," *Fortune,* June, 1956; Internal Revenue Service, *Statistics of Income, 1955—Corporation Income Tax Returns* (Washington, D.C.: Government Printing Office, 1958), pp. 70–71; Bureau of the Census, *Statistical Abstract—1957,* p. 320. Data for 1937, and especially 1955, underestimate the degree of concentration by including in the top 200 corporations some that are in reality part of another corporation's empire; e.g., Western Electric should be counted as a wholly-owned subsidiary of American Telephone and Telegraph. Certain of these adjustments were made for 1955, but these figures must be regarded as conservative estimates.

6. TNEC Monograph No. 29, p. 59; also National Resources Committee, "Basic Characteristics," *The Structure of the American Economy,* Part I (Washington, D.C.: Government Printing Office, 1939), p. 158.

7. Data on these seven types of interlocks are taken from *Report of the Federal Trade Commission on Interlocking Directorates* (Washington, D.C.: Government Printing Office, 1951), pp. 22–36.

8. Relevant data for 1957 calculated from "The *Fortune* Directory," *Fortune,* July and August, 1958. I excluded from the *Fortune* list Western Electric, a subsidiary of a utility, and Joseph E. Seagram & Sons and Shell Oil, both foreign-controlled firms. Richfield Oil was excluded since the majority of its stock is owned by Cities Service and Sinclair Oil. Weyerhaeuser Timber and Singer Manufacturing were excluded since neither is listed on stock exchanges and therefore neither issues any data on internal control, though both are known to be closely owned by the founding families. The Henry J. Kaiser corporations were treated here as one firm.

9. Data for 1937–39 were calculated from TNEC Monograph No. 29, pp. 350–531; 1957 data were calculated from proxy statements and *Moody's Industrials—1957.* A National Industrial Conference Board study of 638 large manufacturing companies, published after my research was completed, applies the line of analysis I used in its examination of companies not in the top 100. In 45 per cent of these corporations, officers held majorities on boards of directors, and they occupied 46 per cent of the board seats. See NICB, *Corporate Directorship Practices,* "Studies in Business Policy," No. 90 (New York: National Industrial Conference Board, 1959).

10. NICB, *Corporate Directorship Practices,* pp. 17–18.

11. *Ibid.,* p. 52; U.S. Senate, Committee on the Judiciary, *Bigness and the Concentration of Economic Power—A Case Study of General Motors Corporation,* Report of the Committee, 84th Cong., 2nd Sess. (Washington, D.C.: Government Printing Office, 1956), p. 55.

12. All data on these and the 100 corporations discussed in this chapter were calculated from proxy statements for 1957 in the Corporate Records Division, Baker Library, Harvard Business School, and from Forms 4, 5, and 6 on file in the Public Reference Room, Securities and Exchange Commission, Washington, D.C. Forms S-1 and 10-K were also used. Only voting stock, common or preferred, is calculated, though preferred is of very little consequence. Stock options held but not exercised were excluded. Included is stock managed by professional representatives sitting on boards—either for personal trusts or holding companies—and directors' beneficial interests in partnerships, trusts, and estates, including the known holdings of their direct families.

13. Robert A. Gordon, *Business Leadership in the Large Corporation* (Washington, D.C.: Brookings Institution, 1945), pp. 32–34.

14. For a discussion of proxy fights, see *Wall Street Journal*, April 30, 1958, p. 1; *New York Times*, March 22, 1959, p. 1 F.

15. Gordon, *op. cit.*, pp. 40–41 ff.

16. David T. Bazelon, "Facts and Fictions of U.S. Capitalism," *The Reporter*, September 17, 1959, pp. 43, 45; John K. Galbraith in *New York Times Book Review*, September 6, 1959, p. 3.

17. Securities and Exchange Commission, *Official Summary of Security Transactions and Holdings*, February, 1957, p. 11.

18. NICB, *Compensation of Top Executives;* and calculations from *Moody's Industrial Manual—1960*.

19. "1,700 Top Executives," *Fortune*, November, 1959, p. 138.

20. Kimmel, *Share Ownership in the U.S.*, pp. 98–99. Kimmel provides very detailed information on the occupational-class affiliations of individual shareholders. The major shortcoming of his survey is the inclusion of an additional 2.13 million unemployed housewives and 130,000 students and preschool children in its figure of 6.49 million shareholders. Housewives and children do not form a socioeconomic class, however, and since only 4.75 million separate families and individuals own stock, it is obvious they must be sharply reduced in number to 520,000 living units if an accurate, noninflated occupational distribution is to be obtained.

21. Butters, *op. cit.*, p. 382; and calculations from "Study 650" (Unpublished data; Survey Research Center, 1957), Table LA-156.

Chapter 5: The Causes of Poverty

1. Max Lerner, *America as a Civilization* (New York: Simon and Schuster, 1957), p. 338.

2. John Kenneth Galbraith, *The Affluent Society* (Boston: Houghton Mifflin Company, 1958), pp. 325 ff.; Talcott Parsons, "A Revised Analytical Approach to the Theory of Social Stratification," *Class, Status*

and Power, ed. Reinhard Bendix and Seymour Martin Lipset (Glencoe, Ill.: The Free Press, 1953), p. 127.

3. Allen, *op. cit.,* p. 213.

4. Seymour Martin Lipset and Natalie Rogoff, "Class and Opportunity in Europe and the United States," *Commentary,* December, 1954, p. 568.

5. Nelson N. Foote and Paul K. Hatt, "Social Mobility and Economic Advancement," *American Economic Review,* May, 1953, pp. 369–70.

6. U.S. Senate, Committee on Labor and Public Service, *Staff Report on Retail Establishments and the Fair Labor Standards Act,* 84th Cong., 2nd Sess. (Washington, D.C.: Government Printing Office, 1956), p. 1.

7. Bureau of Labor Statistics, *Employee Earnings in Retail Trade— October 1956* (Washington, D.C.: Government Printing Office, 1957), p. 1.

8. Bureau of Labor Statistics, *Studies of the Economic Effects of the $1.00 Minimum Wage* (Washington, D.C.: Government Printing Office, 1957), pp. 1, 4, 26.

9. *Current Population Reports,* P-60, No. 27, pp. 4, 27.

10. Goldman, *op. cit.,* p. 436.

11. Conference on Economic Progress, *Full Prosperity for Agriculture* (Washington, D.C.: Conference on Economic Progress, 1955), pp. 25, 97; Hoffman, *op. cit.,* p. 279.

12. For a discussion of this point, see Burkhead, *op. cit.,* pp. 241-47.

13. Calculated from data in *Economic Report of the President— 1958,* pp. 144–46; and *Economic Report of the President—1961,* p. 158. The *Report* for 1961 does not supply the data for calculating real income in special industries.

14. *Monthly Labor Review,* June, 1955, p. 671.

15. U.S. Congress, Joint Committee on the Economic Report, *Characteristics of the Low-Income Population and Related Federal Programs,* 84th Cong., 1st Sess. (Washington, D.C.: Government Printing Office, 1955), p. 6; Selma F. Goldsmith, "Income Distribution . . . ," *op. cit.,* p. 11.

16. Bureau of Labor Statistics, *Employment and Earnings,* March, 1961, p. 7; W. S. Woytinsky, *Employment and Wages in the United States* (New York: Twentieth Century Fund, 1953), pp. 413–14.

17. *Monthly Labor Review,* April, 1956, p. 405.

18. *Current Population Reports,* P-60, No. 30, pp. 4, 36.

19. *Economic Report of the President—1961,* p. 151; *New York Times,* August 10, 1958, p. 36; U.S. Senate, Special Committee on Unemployment Problems, *The Impact of Unemployment in the 1958 Recession,* 86th Cong., 2nd Sess. (Washington, D.C.: Government Printing Office, 1960), pp. 30 ff.

20. U.S. Congress, Joint Committee on the Economic Report, *Hearings on Low-Income Families*, 84th Cong., 1st Sess. (Washington, D.C.: Government Printing Office, 1956), p. 745.

21. Creamer, *op. cit.*, p. 114. Richard A. Lester has shown that less than one-fifth of the wage loss due to total and partial unemployment from 1948 to 1960 was compensated for by regular and emergency unemployment compensation plans. See "The Economic Significance of Unemployment Compensation, 1948–1959," *Review of Economics and Statistics,* November, 1960, pp. 349–72.

22. Lloyd Reynolds and Cynthia Taft, *The Evolution of Wage Structure* (New Haven, Conn.: Yale University Press, 1956); and Harold M. Levinson, *Unionism, Wage Trends, and Income Distribution, 1914–1947* (Ann Arbor, Mich.: University of Michigan Press, 1951), provide material to document this point.

23. Data for lawyers, physicians, and dentists are from *Statistical Abstract—1956*, chart 380; data for educators are from Beardsley Ruml and Stanley G. Tickton, *Teaching Salaries Then and Now* (New York: Fund for the Advancement of Education, 1955); data for other professions are from Harold F. Clark, *Life Earnings in Selected Occupations in the United States* (New York: Harper & Brothers, 1937), and from Census information given in Herman P. Miller, *Income of the American People* (New York: John Wiley & Sons, 1955); data on workers' income by industry are taken from M. Ada Beney, *Wages, Hours, and Employment in the United States, 1914–1936* (New York: National Industrial Conference Board, 1936), and from Census information given in Miller, *op. cit.;* income-tenth range for 1929 is from Leven, *op. cit.,* p. 96; 1935–36 range is from National Resources Committee, *Consumer Incomes in the U.S.,* p. 95; postwar income ranges from *FRB,* July, 1954, p. 700. In obtaining the 1929 and 1935–36 annual incomes of industrial workers, their average weekly incomes were multiplied by 51 and 10 per cent was deducted for 1929, 20 per cent for 1935–36. The basic technique was developed by Harold F. Clark, *op. cit.,* pp. 132–33.

24. George Katona and Janet A. Fisher, "Postwar Changes in the Income of Identical Consumer Units," *Studies in Income and Wealth,* XIII, 72.

25. Kuznets, *op. cit.,* pp. 131–40.

26. Data for 1910 are from Gladys L. Palmer and Ann R. Miller, "The Occupational and Industrial Distribution of Employment, 1910–50," *Manpower in the United States,* ed. William Haber *et al.* (New York: Harper & Brothers, 1954), p. 87; subsequent data are from Conrad and Irene B. Taeuber, *The Changing Population of the United States* (New York: John Wiley & Sons, 1958), pp. 207–8.

27. *FRB,* September, 1958, p. 1052; Selma F. Goldsmith, "Income Distribution . . . ," *op. cit.,* p. 10.

28. See Dorothy S. Brady, "Research on the Size Distribution of Income," *Studies in Income and Wealth,* XIII, 51.

29. For important data supporting the generalizations in this paragraph, see Woytinsky, *Earnings and Social Security,* chap. xiv; and John B. Lansing and James N. Morgan, "Consumer Finances over the Life Cycle," *Consumer Behavior,* ed. Lincoln H. Clark (New York: New York University Press, 1955), II, 36–51.

30. Kuznets, *op. cit.,* p. 143.

31. Woytinsky, *Earnings and Social Security,* pp. 233, 240; *FRB,* August, 1957, p. 892; Janet A. Fisher, "Income, Spending, and Saving Patterns of Consumer Units in Different Age Groups," *Studies in Income and Wealth* (New York: National Bureau of Economic Research, 1952), XV, 82. A thirty-five-year-old member of a lower-income occupational class may be closer in objective economic status to a sixty-year-old member of a "higher" occupational class than to a sixty-year-old member of his own class. Thus, they will be economically similar and a part of that larger configuration, the "lower" or "working" class, which is identical economically if not always occupationally. It would be valuable if the age-income relationship to subjective class consciousness were investigated. It is only after obligations rise that the economic impact of a class position is felt, and until that time conscious class identification may be deferred.

32. U.S. Congress, Joint Committee on the Economic Report, *Characteristics of the Low-Income Population,* p. 122; Social Security Administration, *Illustrative United States Population Projections* (Washington, D.C.: Government Printing Office, 1957), Actuarial Study No. 46, pp. 23–24; *Economic Report of the President—1960,* p. 85.

33. Peter O. Steiner and Robert Dorfman, *The Economic Status of the Aged* (Berkeley, Calif.: University of California Press, 1957), p. 39; *Social Security Bulletin,* December, 1959, p. 14.

34. *Social Security Bulletin,* December, 1959, p. 14; *Public Welfare,* April, 1957, p. 74.

35. *Social Security Bulletin,* March, 1961, p. 1; *FRB,* September, 1958, p. 1055.

36. *Social Security Bulletin,* August, 1955, p. 15.

37. *Ibid.,* March, 1961, p. 32.

38. *Current Population Reports,* P-20, No. 68, p. 2; No. 72, p. 2; No. 75, p. 2; No. 76, p. 4; J. Frederic Dewhurst, *America's Needs and Resources* (New York: Twentieth Century Fund, 1955), p. 57; Woytinsky, *Earnings and Social Security,* p. 50; *New York Times,* August 9, 1959, p. 62.

39. *Monthly Labor Review,* April, 1956, pp. 406 ff.

40. Data for 1939 and 1947 are from Herman P. Miller, "Factors Related to Recent Changes in Income Distribution in the United States," *Review of Economics and Statistics,* August, 1951, p. 218; 1956

data were calculated from *Current Population Reports,* P-20, No. 68, p. 2; No. 81, p. 12.

41. *Current Population Reports,* P-20, No. 96, p. 1.

42. National Bureau of Economic Research, *37th Annual Report,* p. 75; *Current Population Reports,* P-25, No. 165, p. 5.

43. U.S. Congress, Joint Committee on the Economic Report, *Characteristics of the Low-Income Population,* pp. 12, 33.

44. Bureau of Labor Statistics, *Notes on the Economic Status of Negroes in the United States* (Washington, D.C.: Government Printing Office, 1959), pp. 8, 11; *Current Population Reports,* P-25, No. 212, p. 5.

45. U.S. Congress, Joint Committee on the Economic Report, *Characteristics of the Low-Income Population,* pp. 11, 33.

46. National Resources Committee, *Consumer Incomes in the U.S.,* p. 95.

47. *Social Security Bulletin,* May, 1958, p. 1; *Wall Street Journal,* June 4, 1958, p. 1.

48. *Social Security Bulletin,* May, 1958; p. 1; Social Security Administration, *Characteristics of Families Receiving Aid to Dependent Children* (Washington, D.C.: Government Printing Office, 1955), p. 4.

49. *Wall Street Journal,* June 4, 1958; February 24, 26, and March 4, 1959; January 28, 1960; *New York Times,* January 25, 1959—all p. 1.

Chapter 6: The Extent of Poverty

1. Ross and Van den Haag, *op. cit.,* p. 383.

2. Bureau of Labor Statistics, *Handbook of Labor Statistics, 1941 Edition* (Washington, D.C.: Government Printing Office, 1942), Bulletin No. 694, pp. 97–98.

3. Bureau of Labor Statistics, *Workers' Budgets in the United States: City Families and Single Persons, 1946 and 1947* (Washington, D.C.: Government Printing Office, 1948), Bulletin No. 927, p. 2.

4. *Monthly Labor Review,* May, 1952, p. 522.

5. Works Progress Administration [Margaret Loomis Stecker], *Intercity Differences in Costs of Living in March 1935, 59 Cities* (Washington, D.C.: Government Printing Office, 1937), Research Monograph 12, p. xvii.

6. Bureau of Labor Statistics, *Workers' Budgets in the United States . . . 1946 and 1947,* Bulletin No. 927, p. 57. I calculate the cost of a family of seven or more persons at 140 per cent, which gives my data a conservative bias, since the average family in this group has over eight members.

7. *Monthly Labor Review,* May, 1952, p. 520.

8. Bureau of Labor Statistics, *Workers' Budgets in the United States . . . 1946 and 1947,* Bulletin No. 927.

9. *AFL-CIO Collective Bargaining Report,* April, 1956, p. 28; *IUD* [*Industrial Union Department*] *Bulletin,* April, 1960, p. 3.

10. Newel Howland Comish, *The Standard of Living* (New York: The Macmillian Company, 1923), pp. 66–67.

11. Charles S. Wyand, *The Economics of Consumption* (New York: The Macmillan Company, 1937), pp. 459–60.

12. Leven, *op. cit.,* p. 87.

13. Nathan Koffsky, "Farm and Urban Purchasing Power," *Studies in Income and Wealth* (New York: National Bureau of Economic Research, 1949), XI, 172, 175.

14. Mollie Orshansky, "Equivalent Levels of Living: Farm and City," *Studies in Income and Wealth,* XV, 191–92.

15. Data for 1947 were calculated from *Statistical Abstract—1949,* p. 293; 1951 data were calculated from *Current Population Reports,* P-60, No. 12, p. 19; 1957 data were calculated from *Current Population Reports,* P-60, No. 30, p. 21. The 1957 budget is assumed to be $4,500 for a family of four, 10 per cent more than the 1951 budget cost given by the Bureau of Labor Statistics, and about equal to the rise of the Consumer Price Index. This figure is undoubtedly $200–$300 too low. On the basis of less specific data in *FRB,* June, 1948, pp. 651, 656, 48 per cent of the spending units were below the maintenance level and 31 per cent below the emergency level in 1947.

In all calculations, it was sometimes necessary to estimate the number of spending units below the maintenance or emergency level by dividing an income class and the spending units of a given size in it by approximately the income line of the maintenance or emergency level. For example, where a maintenance level was $3,661, it was assumed that three-tenths of the spending units earning between $3,500 and $4,000 were living below the maintenance level. When this sometimes arbitrary income splitting is avoided, as in 1947, and only spending units in the brackets below the maintenance or emergency level for their family sizes are included, about 48 per cent were estimated to have earned less than the maintenance level and about 28 per cent less than the emergency level. Since this estimate is far too conservative, the income-splitting technique is preferable and more accurate—to within one or two percentage points.

In late 1959, the Bureau of Labor Statistics made a preliminary revision of its budget, increasing the standard of absolute consumption about one-fifth over the budget used in my calculations. In twenty large cities, the average income required to meet this standard was $6,084 for a family of four. In 1959, however, 55.6 per cent of all families and unrelated individuals had a money income below that sufficient to provide this standard of living after adjustments for family size were made. The Bureau of Labor Statistics' complete revision will be issued in 1964. See Helen H. Lamale and Margaret S. Stotz, "The

Interim City Worker's Family Budget," *Monthly Labor Review,* August, 1960, pp. 785–808; *Current Population Reports,* P-60, No. 35, p. 25.

16. Data taken from a copy of the speech issued January 30, 1957. It was summarized in the *New York Times,* January 31, 1957, p. 13. Budget information from U.S. Congress, Joint Committee on the Economic Report, *Low-Income Families,* pp. 189 ff. The Interdepartmental Committee kindly allowed me to read its completed report in June, 1958. The preliminary study on which my figures are based appeared in December, 1956, in "The American 'Income Revolution,' " *Dissent,* Winter, 1957, pp. 35–55.

17. Steiner and Dorfman, *op. cit.,* pp. 71, 80; Eleanor M. Snyder, "A Method of Identifying Chronic Low Income Groups from Cross-Section Survey Data," *Studies in Income and Wealth,* XXIII, 333.

18. *Monthly Labor Review,* November, 1939, pp. 1, 166; and February, 1951, p. 153; Miller, *Income of the American People,* pp. 173–86.

19. Taeuber, *op. cit.,* p. 224.

20. *Current Population Reports,* P-60, No. 24, p. 5.

21. *FRB,* June, 1956, p. 570.

22. Data from *Business Week,* June 16, 1956, p. 133.

23. See Gabriel Kolko, "High Pay and Six-Hour Day in Akron," *New Republic,* February 13, 1956, pp. 10–11; *New York Times,* October 4, 1959, p. 86.

24. Calculated from *Economic Report of the President—1958,* pp. 125, 167–68.

25. *Ibid.;* Blanche Bernstein, *The Pattern of Consumer Debt, 1935–36* (New York: National Bureau of Economic Research, 1940), pp. 22, 126.

26. *1960 Survey of Consumer Finances,* p. 160.

27. *Ibid.*

28. Calculated from *FRB,* December, 1951, p. 1516; *Economic Report of the President—1958,* pp. 58, 167–69; *Wall Street Journal,* October 20, 1959, p. 3.

29. Avram Kisselgoff, *Factors Affecting the Demand for Consumer Instalment Sales Credit* (New York: National Bureau of Economic Research, 1952), Technical Paper 7, p. 60.

30. Board of Governors of the Federal Reserve System, *Consumer Instalment Credit: Growth and Import* (Washington, D.C.: Government Printing Office, 1957), Part I, Vol. I, 231–32.

31. For a discussion of these occupational class changes and their significance, see Gabriel Kolko, "Economic Mobility and Social Stratification," *American Journal of Sociology,* July, 1957, pp. 30–38.

32. Joseph Schumpeter, *Capitalism, Socialism, and Democracy* (3rd ed.; New York: Harper & Brothers, 1950), pp. 156–63.

Chapter 7: Income Inequality and Consumption

1. Seymour Martin Lipset and Reinhard Bendix, "Ideological Equalitarianism and Social Mobility in the United States," *Transactions of the Second World Congress of Sociology* (London: International Sociological Association, 1954), II, 50; see also Lipset's "Socialism—Left and Right—East and West," *Confluence,* Summer, 1958, pp. 184–87.

2. Gideon Sjoberg, "Are Social Classes in America Becoming More Rigid?" *American Sociological Review,* December, 1951, p. 780.

3. Kurt Mayer, "Recent Changes in the Class Structure of the United States," *Transactions of the Third World Congress of Sociology* (London: International Sociological Association, 1956), III, 77.

4. Riesman, *op. cit.,* pp. 286 ff.

5. Spengler, *op. cit.,* p. 256.

6. John B. Miner, *Intelligence in the United States* (New York: Springer Publishing Co., 1957), p. 77; see also pp. 29–37. An excellent summary of the literature on the relation of socioeconomic class to IQ, etc., can be found in Seymour B. Sarason and Thomas Gladwin, "Psychological and Cultural Problems in Mental Subnormality: A Review of Research," *American Journal of Mental Deficiency,* May, 1958, pp. 1169–82.

7. Byron S. Hollinshead *et al., Who Should Go to College?* (New York: Columbia University Press, 1952), p. 38; National Manpower Council, *A Policy for Scientific and Professional Manpower* (New York: Columbia University Press, 1953), pp. 79–84.

8. Coleman R. Griffith, "Facilities and Economic Barriers in Education," *Discriminations in Higher Education,* ed. Francis J. Brown *et al.* (Washington, D.C.: American Council on Education, 1951), p. 48; Helen Bertha Goetsch, *Parental Income and College Opportunities* (New York: Teachers College, Columbia University, 1940), p. 87.

9. Educational Testing Service, *Background Factors Relating to College Plans and College Enrollment Among Public High School Students* (Princeton, N.J.: Educational Testing Service, 1957), pp. v–vi.

10. U.S. Congress, Joint Economic Committee, *Characteristics of the Low-Income Population,* p. 54.

11. U.S. Office of Education [Ernest V. Hollis], *Costs of Attending College: A Study of Student Expenditures and Sources of Income* (Washington, D.C.: Government Printing Office, 1957), Office of Education Bulletin 1957, No. 9, pp. 47, 50; *FRB,* June, 1953, p. 11 of reprint including supplementary data; *New York Times,* April 5, 1959, p. 84.

12. Hollinshead, *op. cit.,* p. 138.

13. Dael Wolfle, *America's Resources of Specialized Talent* (New York: Harper & Brothers, 1954), pp. 160, 162.

14. Miner, *op. cit.,* p. 129.

15. Hollis, *op. cit.,* p. 10.

16. Richard H. Ostheimer, *Student Charges and Financing Higher Education* (New York: Columbia University Press, 1953), p. 124; Goetsch, *op cit.,* p. 93.

17. Paul H. Buck, "Who Comes to Harvard?" *Harvard Alumni Bulletin,* January 10, 1948, pp. 314–15.

18. Educational Testing Service, *op. cit.,* p. iv.

19. Hollis, *op. cit.,* p. 22; *New York Times,* April 5, 1959, p. 84; *Wall Street Journal,* May 29, 1961, p. 1; Elmer D. West (ed.), *Background for a National Scholarship Policy* (Washington, D.C.. American Council on Education, 1956), p. 25. The West study is also an excellent survey of the research on the economics of education.

20. William G. Mollenkopf and Robert E. Dear, *An Analysis of Factors Affecting Financial Aid Offers and Awards* (Princeton, N.J.: Educational Testing Service, 1957), pp. 8–9, 20.

21. Richard G. King, "Financial Thresholds to College," *College Board Review,* Spring, 1957, p. 23.

22. See Social Security Administration, *Medical Care and Costs in Relation to Family Income* (2nd ed.; Washington, D.C.: Government Printing Office, 1947), Bureau of Research Memorandum No. 51, p. 177.

23. President's Commission on the Health Needs of the Nation, *America's Health Status, Needs, and Resources* (Washington, D.C.: Government Printing Office, 1953), III, 271.

24. Odin W. Anderson and Jacob J. Feldman, *Family Medical Costs and Voluntary Health Insurance* (New York: McGraw-Hill Book Co., 1956), p. 199.

25. *Industrial Bulletin* [New York State Department of Labor], May, 1959, pp. 7, 10; *Social Security Bulletin,* December, 1959, p. 9; Social Security Administration, *Research and Statistics Note No. 20,* September 21, 1960, p. 5; U.S. Senate, Committee on Labor and Public Welfare, Hearings, *The Aged and Aging in the United States,* 86th Cong., 1st Sess., Part 1 (Washington, D.C.: Government Printing Office, 1959), pp. 24 ff.

26. Anderson, *op. cit.,* p. 37.

27. Social Security Administration, *Medical Care and Costs,* p. 75; President's Commission on Health Needs, *op. cit.,* p. 49.

28. John M. Ellis, "Socio-Economic Differentials in Mortality from Chronic Diseases," *Social Problems,* July, 1957, p. 33; *Newsweek,* March 7, 1960, pp. 78–80. See also E. Gartly Jaco (ed.), *Patients, Physicians and Illness* (Glencoe, Ill.: The Free Press, 1958).

29. Robert E. Clark, "Psychoses, Income, and Occupational Prestige," *American Journal of Sociology,* March, 1949, p. 436; August B. Hollingshead and Fredrick C. Redlich, *Social Class and Mental Illness* (New York: John Wiley & Sons, 1958), pp. 210, 309.

30. Bureau of the Census, *1950 United States Census of Housing—*

U.S. Summary (Washington, D.C.: Government Printing Office, 1953), pp. xxxiii–xxxv; Bureau of the Census, *1956 National Housing Inventory* (Washington, D.C.: Government Printing Office, 1959), III, Part 1, 16; *Labor's Economic Review,* September, 1959, pp. 49–50; Bureau of the Census, *1960 Census of Housing: Advance Reports—Housing Characteristics,* April, 1961, p. 5.

31. Bureau of the Census, *National Housing Inventory,* III, Part 1, 35; *FRB,* September, 1959, pp. 1107–9.

32. National Housing Conference, *The Housing Yearbook—1957* (Washington, D.C.: National Housing Conference, 1957), p. 21; *FRB,* August, 1956, p. 822.

33. Charles Abrams, "Public Housing Myths," *New Leader,* July 25, 1955, p. 3; *New York Times,* January 31, 1957, p. 1. At various times, so-called slums have in reality consisted of decent low-income houses, which, because they are in prime real-estate locations, have been ripped down to make way for upper-income housing. See, for example, Herbert J. Gans, "The Human Implications of Current Redevelopment and Relocation Planning," *Journal of the American Institute of Planners,* February, 1959.

34. *FRB,* July, 1959, p. 717; National Resources Committee, *Family Expenditures in the U.S.,* p. 4; Bureau of Labor Statistics, *Family Spending and Saving in Wartime,* p. 76.

35. National Resources Committee, *Family Expenditures in the U.S.,* p. 27; *FRB,* May, 1955, p. 475.

36. *FRB,* May, 1955, p. 477.

37. Bureau of the Census, *Travel Survey—1957* (Washington, D.C.: Government Printing Office, 1958), p. 3; *Current Population Reports,* P-20, No. 95, p. 2.

38. *Wall Street Journal,* November 4, 1959, p. 3.

39. *Business Week,* November 15, 1958, p. 60.

40. "The $250,000 House," *Fortune,* October, 1955, pp. 133–34.

41. *Wall Street Journal,* November 26, 1957, p. 1; see also August 18, 26, 30, and September 9, 1955; October 16, 1956; July 18, 1957; September 8, 1959; March 21, 1960.

42. The percentage allocation of spending-unit income is given for each income class in *Statistical Abstract—1957,* p. 307.

Chapter 8: The Quality of Economic Life: Myth and Reality

1. Louis Hartz, *The Liberal Tradition in America* (New York: Harcourt, Brace & Company, 1955), p. 206.

2. Galbraith, *op. cit.,* p. 3.

Bibliography

The following standard publications were utilized throughout this book, but individual volumes or issues are not listed in the bibliography below. Specific citations appear in the footnotes. The government sources are: *Federal Reserve Bulletin, Monthly Labor Review, Statistics of Income, Social Security Bulletin, Survey of Current Business, Statistical Abstracts, Economic Reports of the President,* and *Current Population Reports,* Series P-20, 25, 50, and 60. Nongovernment publications include: *Moody's Industrials, Wall Street Journal, New York Times, Business Week,* and various corporation proxies.

Books

ALLEN, FREDERICK LEWIS. *The Big Change.* New York: Harper & Brothers, 1952.

ANDERSON, ODIN W., and FELDMAN, JACOB J. *Family Medical Costs and Voluntary Health Insurance.* New York: McGraw-Hill Book Company, 1956.

BENEY, M. ADA. *Wages, Hours, and Employment in the United States, 1914–1936.* New York: National Industrial Conference Board, 1936.

BERLE, ADOLF A., JR., *Power Without Property.* New York: Harcourt, Brace & Company, 1959.

———. *The 20th Century Capitalist Revolution.* New York: Harcourt, Brace & Company, 1954.

BERNSTEIN, BLANCHE. *The Pattern of Consumer Debt, 1935–36.* New York: National Bureau of Economic Research, 1940.

BLAKEY, ROY G. and GLADYS C. *The Federal Income Tax.* New York: Longmans, Green & Co., 1940.

BUTTERS, J. KEITH, *et al. Effects of Taxation—Investment by Individuals.* Boston: Harvard Business School, 1953.

CLARK, HAROLD F. *Life Earnings in Selected Occupations in the United States.* New York: Harper & Brothers, 1937.

CLOUGH, SHEPARD B. *The American Way: The Economic Basis of Our Civilization.* New York: Thomas Y. Crowell Company, 1953.

COCHRAN, THOMAS C. *The American Business System: A Historical Perspective.* Cambridge, Mass.: Harvard University Press, 1957.

COMISH, NEWEL HOWLAND. *The Standard of Living.* New York: The Macmillan Company, 1923.

CREAMER, DANIEL. *Personal Income During Business Cycles.* Princeton, N.J.: Princeton University Press, 1956.

CRUM, WILLIAM, *et al. Fiscal Planning for Total War.* New York: National Bureau of Economic Research, 1942.

DEWHURST, J. FREDERIC. *America's Needs and Resources.* New York: Twentieth Century Fund, 1955.

DUESENBERRY, JAMES S. *Income, Saving and the Theory of Consumer Behavior.* Cambridge, Mass.: Harvard University Press, 1949.

GALBRAITH, JOHN KENNETH. *The Affluent Society.* Boston: Houghton Mifflin Company, 1958.

GOETSCH, HELEN BERTHA. *Parental Income and College Opportunities.* New York: Teachers College, Columbia University, 1940.

GOLDMAN, ERIC F. *Rendezvous with Destiny.* New York: Alfred A. Knopf, 1952.

GOLDSMITH, RAYMOND W. *A Study of Saving in the United States.* 3 vols. Princeton, N.J.: Princeton University Press, 1955.

GORDON, ROBERT A. *Business Leadership in the Large Corporation.* Washington, D.C.: Brookings Institution, 1945.

HARBRECHT, PAUL P. *Pension Funds and Economic Power.* New York: Twentieth Century Fund, 1959.

HARTZ, LOUIS. *The Liberal Tradition in America.* New York: Harcourt, Brace & Company, 1955.

HOLLAND, DANIEL M. *The Income-Tax Burden on Stockholders.* Princeton, N.J.: Princeton University Press, 1958.

HOLLINGSHEAD, AUGUST B., and REDLICH, FREDRICK C. *Social Class and Mental Illness.* New York: John Wiley & Sons, 1958.

HOLLINSHEAD, BYRON S., *et al. Who Should Go to College?* New York: Columbia University Press, 1952.

JACO, E. GARTLY (ed.). *Patients, Physicians and Illness.* Glencoe, Ill.: The Free Press, 1958.

KIMMEL, LEWIS H. *Share Ownership in the United States.* Washington, D.C.: Brookings Institution, 1952.

———. *Taxes and Economic Incentives.* Washington, D.C.: Brookings Institution, 1950.

KUZNETS, SIMON. *Shares of Upper Income Groups in Income and Savings.* New York: National Bureau of Economic Research, 1953.

LERNER, MAX. *America as a Civilization.* New York: Simon and Schuster, 1957.

LESCOHIER, DON D. *Working Conditions.* (*History of Labor in the United States,* ed. JOHN R. COMMONS, Vol. III.) New York: The Macmillan Company, 1935.

LEVEN, MAURICE, *et al. America's Capacity to Consume.* Washington, D.C.: Brookings Institution, 1934.

LEVINSON, HAROLD M. *Unionism, Wage Trends, and Income Distribution, 1914–1947.* Ann Arbor, Mich.: University of Michigan, 1951.

LILIENTHAL, DAVID E. *Big Business: A New Era.* New York: Harper & Brothers, 1953.

MILLER, HERMAN P. *Income of the American People.* New York: John Wiley & Sons, 1955.

MINER, JOHN B. *Intelligence in the United States.* New York: Springer Publishing Co., 1957.

MITCHELL, WESLEY C., *et al. Income in the United States, 1910–1918.* 2 vols. New York: National Bureau of Economic Research, 1921.

NATIONAL INDUSTRIAL CONFERENCE BOARD. *Studies in Enterprise and Social Progress.* New York: National Industrial Conference Board, 1939.

NATIONAL MANPOWER COUNCIL. *A Policy of Scientific and Professional Manpower.* New York: Columbia University Press, 1953.

OSTHEIMER, RICHARD H. *Student Charges and Financing Higher Education.* New York: Columbia University Press, 1953.

PAUL, RANDOLPH. *Taxation in the United States.* Boston: Little, Brown & Co., 1954.

REYNOLDS, LLOYD, and TAFT, CYNTHIA. *The Evolution of Wage Structure.* New Haven, Conn.: Yale University Press, 1956.

RIESMAN, DAVID, *et al. The Lonely Crowd.* New York: Doubleday & Company, 1953.

ROSS, RALPH, and VAN DEN HAAG, ERNEST. *The Fabric of Society: An Introduction to the Social Sciences.* New York: Harcourt, Brace & Company, 1957.

RUML, BEARDSLEY, and TICKTON, STANLEY G. *Teaching Salaries Then and Now.* New York: Fund for the Advancement of Education, 1955.

SCHUMPETER, JOSEPH. *Capitalism, Socialism, and Democracy.* 3rd ed. New York: Harper & Brothers, 1950.

SELTZER, LAWRENCE H. *The Nature and Tax Treatment of Capital*

Gains and Losses. New York. National Bureau of Economic Research, 1951.

STEINER, PETER O., and DORFMAN, ROBERT. *The Economic Status of the Aged.* Berkeley, Calif.: University of California Press, 1957.

SURVEY RESEARCH CENTER. *1960 Survey of Consumer Finances.* Ann Arbor, Mich.: Survey Research Center, 1960.

TAEUBER, CONRAD and IRENE. *The Changing Population of the United States.* New York: John Wiley & Sons, 1958.

WOLFLE, DAEL. *America's Resources of Specialized Talent.* New York: Harper & Brothers, 1954.

WOYTINSKY, W. S. *Earnings and Social Security in the United States.* Washington, D.C.: Social Science Research Council, 1943.

———. *Employment and Wages in the United States.* New York: Twentieth Century Fund, 1953.

WYAND, CHARLES S. *The Economics of Consumption.* New York: The Macmillan Company, 1937.

Government Publications

BUREAU OF THE CENSUS, DEPARTMENT OF COMMERCE. *1950 United States Census of Housing—U.S. Summary.* Washington, D.C.: Government Printing Office, 1953.

———. *1956 National Housing Inventory.* Vol. III, Part 1. Washington, D.C.: Government Printing Office, 1959.

———. *1960 Census of Housing: Advance Reports—Housing Characteristics.* Washington, D.C.: Government Printing Office, April, 1961.

———. *Travel Survey—1957.* Washington, D.C.: Government Printing Office, 1958.

BUREAU OF INTERNAL REVENUE, DEPARTMENT OF THE TREASURY. *The Audit Control Program: A Summary of Preliminary Results.* Washington, D.C.: Government Printing Office, 1951.

BUREAU OF LABOR STATISTICS, DEPARTMENT OF LABOR. *Employee Earnings in Retail Trade—October 1956.* Washington, D.C.: Government Printing Office, 1957.

———. *Family Spending and Saving in Wartime.* Bulletin No. 822. Washington, D.C.: Government Printing Office, 1945.

———. *Handbook of Labor Statistics, 1941 Edition.* Bulletin No. 694. Washington, D.C.: Government Printing Office, 1942.

———. *Notes on the Economic Status of Negroes in the United States.* Washington, D.C.: Government Printing Office, 1959.

————. *Studies of the Economic Effects of the $1.00 Minimum Wage.* Washington, D.C.: Government Printing Office, 1957.

————. *Workers' Budgets in the United States: City Families and Single Persons, 1946 and 1947.* Bulletin No. 927. Washington, D.C.: Government Printing Office, 1948.

DEPARTMENT OF AGRICULTURE. *1957 Agricultural Outlook Charts.* Washington, D.C.: Government Printing Office, 1956.

FEDERAL RESERVE SYSTEM, BOARD OF GOVERNORS. *Consumer Instalment Credit: Growth and Import.* Part I, Vol. I. Washington, D.C.: Government Printing Office, 1957.

FEDERAL TRADE COMMISSION. *Report of the Federal Trade Commission on Interlocking Directorates.* Washington, D.C.: Government Printing Office, 1951.

NATIONAL RESOURCES COMMITTEE. *Consumer Expenditures in the United States.* Washington, D.C.: Government Printing Office, 1939.

————. *Consumer Incomes in the United States.* Washington, D.C.: Government Printing Office, 1938.

————. *The Structure of the American Economy—Part I, Basic Characteristics.* Washington, D.C.: Government Printing Office, 1939.

OFFICE OF BUSINESS ECONOMICS, DEPARTMENT OF COMMERCE. *Income Distribution in the United States, 1944–1950.* Washington, D.C.: Government Printing Office, 1953.

————. *National Income, 1954.* Washington, D.C.: Government Printing Office, 1954.

————. *U.S. Income and Output.* Washington, D.C.: Government Printing Office, 1958.

OFFICE OF EDUCATION [Ernest V. Hollis]. *Costs of Attending College: A Study of Student Expenditures and Sources of Income.* Office of Education Bulletin 1957, No. 9. Washington, D.C.: Government Printing Office, 1957.

PRESIDENT'S COMMISSION ON THE HEALTH NEEDS OF THE NATION. *America's Health Status, Needs, and Resources.* Vol. III. Washington, D.C.: Government Printing Office, 1953.

SOCIAL SECURITY ADMINISTRATION. *Characteristics of Families Receiving Aid to Dependent Children.* Washington, D.C.: Government Printing Office, 1955.

————. *Illustrative United States Population Projections.* Actuarial Study No. 46. Washington, D.C.: Government Printing Office, 1957.

————. *Medical Care and Costs in Relation to Family Income.* Bureau of Research Memorandum No. 51. Washington, D.C.: Government Printing Office, 1947.

————. *Research and Statistics Note No. 20.* Washington, D.C.: Government Printing Office, 1960.

TEMPORARY NATIONAL ECONOMIC COMMITTEE. *Who Pays the Taxes?* Monograph No. 3. Washington, D.C.: Government Printing Office, 1940.

————. *Concentration and Composition of Individual Incomes, 1918–1937.* Monograph No. 4. Washington, D.C.: Government Printing Office, 1940.

————. *The Distribution of Ownership in the 200 Largest Nonfinancial Corporations.* Monograph No. 29. Washington, D.C.: Government Printing Office, 1940.

————. *Survey of Shareholdings in 1,710 Corporations with Securities Listed on a National Securities Exchange.* Monograph No. 30. Washington, D.C.: Government Printing Office, 1941.

U.S. CONGRESS, JOINT COMMITTEE ON THE ECONOMIC REPORT. *Characteristics of the Low-Income Population and Related Federal Programs.* 84th Cong., 1st Sess. Washington, D.C.: Government Printing Office, 1955.

————. *Hearings on Low-Income Families.* 84th Cong., 1st Sess. Washington, D.C.: Government Printing Office, 1956.

————. *Report on Productivity, Prices, and Income.* 85th Cong., 1st Sess. Washington, D.C.: Government Printing Office, 1957.

U.S. SENATE, COMMITTEE ON BANKING AND CURRENCY. *Income and Housing.* 85th Cong., 1st Sess. Washington, D.C.: Government Printing Office, 1957.

————, COMMITTEE ON THE JUDICIARY. *Bigness and the Concentration of Economic Power—A Case Study of General Motors Corporation.* Report of the Committee, 84th Cong., 2nd Sess. Washington, D.C.: Government Printing Office, 1956.

————, *Study of Administered Prices in the Steel Industry.* Report of the Committee. 85th Cong., 2nd Sess. Washington, D.C.: Government Printing Office, 1958.

————, COMMITTEE ON LABOR AND PUBLIC SERVICE. *Staff Report on Retail Establishments and the Fair Labor Standards Act.* 84th Cong., 2nd Sess. Washington, D.C.: Government Printing Office, 1956.

————, COMMITTEE ON LABOR AND PUBLIC WELFARE. *The Aged and Aging in the United States.* 86th Cong., 1st Sess. Part 1. Washington, D.C.: Government Printing Office, 1959.

————, SPECIAL COMMITTEE ON UNEMPLOYMENT PROBLEMS. *The Impact of Unemployment in the 1958 Recession.* 86th Cong., 2nd Sess. Washington, D.C.: Government Printing Office, 1960.

WORKS PROGRESS ADMINISTRATION [MARGARET LOOMIS STECKER]. *Inter-city Differences in Costs of Living in March 1935, 59 Cities.* Research Monograph 12. Washington, D.C.: Government Printing Office, 1937.

————. *Quantity Budgets for Basic Maintenance and Emergency Standards of Living.* Research Bulletin, Ser. I, No. 21. Washington, D.C.: Government Printing Office, 1936.

Pamphlets

CONFERENCE ON ECONOMIC PROGRESS. *Full Prosperity for Agriculture.* Washington, D.C.: Conference on Economic Progress, 1955.

CRUM, WILLIAM L. *The Distribution of Wealth.* Research Studies No. 13. Boston: Harvard Business School, 1935.

EDUCATIONAL TESTING SERVICE. *Background Factors Relating to College Plans and College Enrollment Among Public High School Students.* Princeton, N.J.: Educational Testing Service, 1957.

FALK, I. S., *et al. The Incidence of Illness and the Receipt and Costs of Medical Care Among Representative Families, 1928–1931.* Washington, D.C.: Committee on the Costs of Medical Care, 1933.

KISSELGOFF, AVRAM. *Factors Affecting the Demand for Consumer Instalment Sales Credit.* Technical Paper 7. New York: National Bureau of Economic Research, 1952.

MOLLENKOPF, WILLIAM G., and DEAR, ROBERT E. *An Analysis of Factors Affecting Financial Aid Offers and Awards.* Princeton, N.J.: Educational Testing Service, 1957.

NATIONAL BUREAU OF ECONOMIC RESEARCH. *The National Economic Accounts of the United States.* Washington, D.C.: Government Printing Office, 1957.

NATIONAL HOUSING CONFERENCE. *The Housing Yearbook—1957.* Washington, D.C.: National Housing Conference, 1957.

NATIONAL INDUSTRIAL CONFERENCE BOARD. *Compensation of Top Executives.* Studies in Personnel Policy, No. 173. New York: National Industrial Conference Board, 1959.

————. *Corporate Directorship Practices.* Studies in Business Policy, No. 90. New York: National Industrial Conference Board, 1959.

POSTON, CHARLES F. *Restricted Stock Options for Management.* Chapel Hill, N.C.: School of Business Administration, University of North Carolina, 1960.

POTTER, DAVID M. (ed.). *People's Capitalism.* New York: The Advertising Council, 1957.

SELTZER, LAWRENCE H. *Interest as a Source of Personal Income and Tax Revenue.* Occasional Paper 51. New York: National Bureau of Economic Research, 1955.

TAX FOUNDATION. *Allocation of the Tax Burden by Income Class.* New York: Tax Foundation, 1960.

———. *Federal Excise Taxes.* New York: Tax Foundation, 1956.

———. *Fiscal Facts for '58.* New York: Tax Foundation, 1958.

———. *Reexamining the Federal Corporation Income Tax.* New York: Tax Foundation, 1958.

TILOVE, ROBERT. *Pension Funds and Economic Freedom.* New York: Fund for the Republic, 1959.

WEST, ELMER D. (ed.). *Background of a National Scholarship Policy.* Washington, D.C.: American Council on Education, 1956.

Articles

ABRAMS, CHARLES. "Public Housing Myths," *New Leader,* XXXVIII (July 25, 1955), 3–6.

BAZELON, DAVID T. "Facts and Fictions of U.S. Capitalism," *The Reporter,* XXI (September 17, 1959), 43–48.

BENDINER, ROBERT. "Credit Cards: The Thirty-Day Tycoons," *The Reporter,* XX (February 5, 1959), 26–30.

BERMAN, HARVEY S. "He's on an Expense Account," *Challenge,* IV (March, 1956), 55–58.

BRADY, DOROTHY S. "Research on the Size Distribution of Income," *Studies in Income and Wealth.* XIII. New York: National Bureau of Economic Research, 1951, 3–55.

BUCK, PAUL H. "Who Comes to Harvard?" *Harvard Alumni Bulletin,* L (January 10, 1948), 313–17.

BURKHEAD, JESSE. "Living Standards and Productivity," *Review of Economics and Statistics,* XXXIII (August, 1951), 241–47.

CARTTER, ALLAN M. "Income Shares of the Upper Income Groups in Great Britain and the United States," *American Economic Review,* XLIV (December, 1954), 875–83.

CENTERS, RICHARD, and CANTRIL, HADLEY. "Income Satisfaction and Income Aspiration," *Journal of Abnormal and Social Psychology,* XLI (January, 1946), 64–69.

CLARK, ROBERT E. "Psychoses, Income, and Occupational Prestige," *American Journal of Sociology,* LIV (March, 1949), 433–40.

EISENSTEIN, LOUIS. "The Rise and Decline of the Estate Tax," in U.S. SENATE, JOINT COMMITTEE ON THE ECONOMIC REPORT. *Federal Tax*

Policy for Economic Growth and Stability. 84th Cong., 1st Sess. Washington, D.C.: Government Printing Office, 1955, pp. 819–46.

ELLIS, JOHN M. "Socio-Economic Differentials in Mortality from Chronic Diseases," *Social Problems,* V (July, 1957), 30–36.

"Expense Account Scandal," *U.S. News & World Report,* XLVIII (January 25, 1960), 50–56.

"Expense Accounts," *Harvard Business Review,* XXXVIII (March–April, 1960), 6–16.

"Expense Accounts: A $5-Billion Tax Deduction, and Growing," *U.S. News & World Report,* XLIII (August 16, 1957), 83–88.

FISHER, JANET A. "Income, Spending, and Saving Patterns of Consumer Units in Different Age Groups," *Studies in Income and Wealth.* XV. New York: National Bureau of Economic Research, 1952, 75–102.

FOOTE, NELSON N., and HATT, PAUL K. "Social Mobility and Economic Advancement," *American Economic Review,* XLIII (May, 1953), 364–78.

GANS, HERBERT J. "The Human Implications of Current Redevelopment and Relocation Planning," *Journal of the American Institute of Planners,* XXV (February, 1959).

GOLDSMITH, RAYMOND W. "Trends and Structural Changes in Savings in the Twentieth Century," *Savings in the Modern Economy,* ed. WALTER W. HELLER *et al.* Minneapolis, Minn.: University of Minnesota Press, 1953, pp. 133–51.

GOLDSMITH, SELMA F. "Appraisal of Basic Data Available for Constructing Income Size Distributions," *Studies in Income and Wealth.* XIII. New York: National Bureau of Economic Research, 1951, 267–373.

———. "Income Distribution by Size—1955–58," *Survey of Current Business,* XXXIX (April, 1959), 9–16.

———. "The Relation of Census Income Distribution Statistics to Other Income Data," *Studies in Income and Wealth.* XXIII. New York: National Bureau of Economic Research, 1958, 65–107.

———, *et al.* "Size Distribution of Income Since the Mid-Thirties," *Review of Economics and Statistics,* XXXVI (February, 1954), 1–32.

GRIFFITH, COLEMAN R. "Facilities and Economic Barriers in Education," *Discriminations in Higher Education,* ed. FRANCIS J. BROWN *et al.* Washington, D.C.: American Council on Education, 1951, pp. 44–49.

HAVEMANN, ERNEST. "The Expense Account Aristocracy," *Life,* XXXIV (March 9, 1953), 140–42.

HELLMUTH, WILLIAM F., JR. "The Corporate Income Tax Base," in U.S. HOUSE OF REPRESENTATIVES, COMMITTEE ON WAYS AND MEANS.

Tax Revision Compendium. 86th Cong., 1st Sess. I. Washington, D.C.: Government Printing Office, 1959, 283–316.

HENLE, PETER. "How Workers Look at Tax Problems," *Income Tax Differentials.* Princeton, N.J.: Tax Institute, 1958, pp. 82–94.

HOFFMAN, SHIRLEY S. "Agriculture as a Buyer," *Business Record,* XVI (June, 1959), 278–80.

HOLLAND, DANIEL M. "Unreporting of Dividends and Interest on Tax Returns," in U.S. HOUSE OF REPRESENTATIVES, COMMITTEE ON WAYS AND MEANS. *Tax Revision Compendium.* 86th Cong. 1st Sess. II. Washington, D.C.: Government Printing Office, 1959, 1397–1438.

——, and KAHN, C. HARRY. "Comparison of Personal and Taxable Income," in U.S. SENATE, JOINT COMMITTEE ON THE ECONOMIC REPORT. *Federal Tax Policy for Economic Growth and Stability.* 84th Cong., 1st Sess. Washington, D.C.: Government Printing Office, 1955, pp. 313–37.

HOLMES, GEORGE K. "The Concentration of Wealth," *Political Science Quarterly,* VIII (December, 1893), 589–600.

KAHN, C. HARRY. "Coverage of Entrepreneurial Income on Federal Tax Returns," in U.S. HOUSE OF REPRESENTATIVES, COMMITTEE ON WAYS AND MEANS. *Tax Revision Compendium.* 86th Cong., 1st Sess. II. Washington, D.C.: Government Printing Office, 1959, 1439–61.

KATONA, GEORGE, *et al.* "Stock Ownership Among American Families," *Michigan Business Review,* V (January, 1953), 12–15.

——, and FISHER, JANET A. "Postwar Changes in the Income of Identical Consumer Units," *Studies in Income and Wealth.* XIII. New York: National Bureau of Economic Research, 1951, 62–119.

KING, RICHARD G. "Financial Thresholds to College," *College Board Review,* XI (Spring, 1957), 22–24.

KOFFSKY, NATHAN. "Farm and Urban Purchasing Power," *Studies in Income and Wealth.* XI. New York: National Bureau of Economic Research, 1949, 156–78.

——, and LEAR, JEANNE E. "Size Distribution of Farm Operators' Income in 1946," *Studies in Income and Wealth.* XIII. New York: National Bureau of Economic Research, 1951, 220–58.

KOLKO, GABRIEL. "The American 'Income Revolution,'" *Dissent,* IV (Winter, 1957), 35–55.

——. "Economic Mobility and Social Stratification," *American Journal of Sociology,* LXIII (July, 1957), 30–38.

——. "High Pay and a Six-Hour Day in Akron," *New Republic,* CXXXIV (February 13, 1956), 10–11.

LAMPMAN, ROBERT J. "Changes in the Share of Wealth Held by Top

Wealth-Holders, 1922–1956," *Review of Economics and Statistics,* XLI (November, 1959), 379–92.

LANSING, JOHN B., and MORGAN, JAMES N. "Consumer Finances over the Life Cycle," in *Consumer Behavior,* ed. LINCOLN H. CLARK. II New York: New York University Press, 1955, 36–51.

LESTER, RICHARD A. "The Economic Significance of Unemployment Compensation, 1948–1959," *Review of Economics and Statistics,* XLII (November, 1960), 349–72.

LIPSET, SEYMOUR MARTIN. "Socialism—Left and Right—East and West," *Confluence,* VII (Summer, 1958), 173–92.

———, and BENDIX, REINHARD. "Ideological Equalitarianism and Social Mobility in the United States," *Transactions of the Second World Congress of Sociology.* II. London: International Sociological Association, 1954, 34–54.

———, and ROGOFF, NATALIE. "Class and Opportunity in Europe and the United States," *Commentary,* XVIII (December, 1954), 562–68.

MAYER, KURT. "Recent Changes in the Class Structure of the United States," *Transactions of the Third World Congress of Sociology.* III. London: International Sociological Association, 66–80.

MILLER, HERMAN P. "Factors Related to Recent Changes in Income Distribution in the United States," *Review of Economics and Statistics,* XXXIII (August, 1951), 214–18.

ORSHANSKY, MOLLIE. "Equivalent Levels of Living: Farm and City," *Studies in Income and Wealth.* XV. New York: National Bureau of Economic Research, 1952, 175–200.

PALMER, GLADYS L., and MILLER, ANN R. "The Occupational and Industrial Distribution of Employment, 1910–50," *Manpower in the United States,* ed. WILLIAM HABER *et al.* New York: Harper & Brothers, 1954, pp. 83–92.

PARSONS, TALCOTT. "A Revised Analytical Approach to the Theory of Social Stratification," *Class, Status and Power,* ed. REINHARD BENDIX and SEYMOUR MARTIN LIPSET. Glencoe, Ill.: The Free Press, 1953, pp. 92–128.

PATTON, ARCH. "Executive Compensation: Tax Gimmicks vs. Incentives," *Harvard Business Review,* XXXI (November–December, 1953), 113–19.

PECHMAN, JOSEPH A. "What Would a Comprehensive Individual Income Tax Yield?" *Tex Revision Compendium.* 86th Cong., 1st Sess. I. Washington, D.C.: Government Printing Office, 1959, 251–82.

PETERSEN, WILLIAM. "Is America Still the Land of Opportunity?" *Commentary,* XVI (November, 1953), 477–86.

RASKIN, A. H. " 'Town Meeting' of the Shareholders," *New York Times Magazine,* May 12, 1957, p. 15.

ROTHSCHILD, V. HENRY, and SOBERNHEIM, RUDOLF. "Expense Accounts for Executives," *Yale Law Journal,* LXVII (July, 1958).

SARASON, SEYMOUR B., and GLADWIN, THOMAS. "Psychological and Cultural Problems in Mental Subnormality: A Review of Research," *American Journal of Mental Deficiency,* LXII (May, 1958), 1115–1307.

SCHULMAN, ROBERT. "Tax Differentials in Executive Compensation," *Income Tax Differentials.* Princeton, N.J.: Tax Institute, 1958, pp. 67–81.

SJOBERG, GIDEON. "Are Social Classes in America Becoming More Rigid?" *American Sociological Review,* XVI (December, 1951), 775–83.

SMYTH, RICHARD C. "Bonus Plans for Executives," *Harvard Business Review,* XXXVII (July–August, 1959), 66–74.

SNYDER, ELEANOR M. "A Method of Identifying Chronic Low Income Groups from Cross-Section Survey Data," *Studies in Income and Wealth.* XXIII. New York: National Bureau of Economic Research, 1958, 321–44.

SPENGLER, JOSEPH J. "Changes in Income Distribution and Social Stratification: A Note," *American Journal of Sociology,* LIX (November, 1953), 247–59.

STOCKER, FREDERICK D., and ELLICKSON, JOHN G. "How Fully Do Farmers Report Their Incomes?" *National Tax Journal,* XII (June, 1959), 116–26.

SURREY, STANLEY S. "The Congress and the Tax Lobbyist—How Special Tax Provisions Get Enacted," *Harvard Law Review,* LXX (May, 1957), 1145–82.

WASSON, ROBERT; HURWITZ, ABNER; and SCHWEIGER, IRVING. "Field Surveys of Consumer Income—An Appraisal," *Studies in Income and Wealth.* XIII. New York: National Bureau of Economic Research, 1951, 482–554.

WHYTE, WILLIAM H. "The Cadillac Phenomenon," *Fortune,* LI (February, 1955), 106–11.

WORMSER, RENÉ A. "How to Save Money by Giving It Away," *U.S. News & World Report,* XLI (December 28, 1956), 106–39.

Index